W9-DFM-907

Thomas Hughes

Twayne's English Authors Series

Herbert Sussman, Editor
Northeastern University

TEAS 387

THOMAS HUGHES
Photograph from J. Llewelyn Davies, ed.,
The Working Men's College 1854–1904
(London: Macmillan, 1904).

Thomas Hughes

By George J. Worth
University of Kansas

Twayne Publishers • *Boston*

Thomas Hughes

George J. Worth

Copyright © 1984 by G. K. Hall & Company
All Rights Reserved
Published by Twayne Publishers
A Division of G. K. Hall & Company
70 Lincoln Street
Boston, Massachusetts 02111

Book Production by Marne B. Sultz

Book Design by Barbara Anderson

Printed on permanent/durable acid-free
paper and bound in the United States of
America.

Library of Congress Cataloging in Publication Data

Worth, George J. (George John), 1929–
    Thomas Hughes.

    (Twayne's English authors series; TEAS 387)
    Bibliography: p. 134
    Includes index.
    1. Hughes, Thomas, 1822–1896—
Criticism and interpretation.
I. Title.   II. Series.
PR4809.H8Z95   1984   823′.8   84-4494
ISBN 0-8057-6873-4

Contents

About the Author

George J. Worth earned the A.B. and A.M. degrees at the University of Chicago and the Ph.D. at the University of Illinois at Urbana-Champaign. Since 1955 he has been a member of the Department of English at the University of Kansas, serving as chairman from 1963 until 1979. His many publications in Victorian literature include an earlier volume in the Twayne English Authors Series, *William Harrison Ainsworth* (1972), and two other books: *James Hannay: His Life and Works* (1964) and *Dickensian Melodrama* (1978).

Preface

No single book of moderate length can do justice to the many achievements of Thomas Hughes (1822–1896). In a richly productive career extending over nearly half a century, he made his distinctive mark in several spheres of Victorian life: as a lawyer, a legislator, and a judge; as a leading middle-class proponent of such working-class movements as cooperation and trade unionism; as a spokesman for a variety of other important social, political, religious, and educational movements; as an advocate of close Anglo-American relations; and, of course, as a man of letters of some prominence.

It is on Thomas Hughes as an author that this study will concentrate, but such a restriction of its subject raises some questions that must be answered, or at least confronted. Hughes started writing for publication while still in his twenties and—seemingly, at least—rarely laid down his pen for the next fifty years or so. Inevitably much of this enormous volume of work was ephemeral, and a great deal of it was not reprinted in book form. We shall have to treat it selectively, slighting or ignoring altogether that considerable portion which is of relatively little interest. Also, Hughes's career as an author took a peculiar course: he achieved fame before he was thirty-five with *Tom Brown's School Days* and never came close to equaling this spectacular success in four more busy decades of writing. The work that came later may appear to have been one long anticlimax, but that is not necessarily an accurate or a fair verdict and it will need to be scrutinized carefully. Finally, though Hughes could be as relaxed, genial, and whimsical as the best nineteenth-century essayists or writers of fiction, his most characteristic work cannot be usefully read simply as belles-lettres. In spite of ourselves, therefore, it is incumbent on us to give some attention to Hughes's nonliterary activities and beliefs to the very considerable extent that they impinged on his writing.

It may be well before beginning to state two propositions that underlie much of the following argument. First, though Hughes was by no stretch of the imagination a great writer, he has been unjustly neglected and underrated. Second, to a surprising degree all his literary work is of a piece; so that, for example, it is impossible to savor properly a novel like *Tom Brown's School Days* without any knowledge of his nonfiction.

If this study moves readers to search out some of that work, it will have achieved its primary purpose. If it encourages a few of them to pursue their own investigations beyond what it has been able to accomplish, or beyond what they will find in Mack and Armytage's excellent biography or the other sources listed in the Notes and References and the Selected Bibliography, that will be a most welcome bonus.

George J. Worth

University of Kansas

Acknowledgments

I want to thank the University of Kansas for its continuing confidence in my work, expressed most recently by the four grants from the General Research Fund and the timely sabbatical leave that enabled me to complete this study right on schedule.

Not even a major renovation that threatened to throw the University's Watson Library into total disarray during two years in which I made heavy demands on its holdings and facilities kept the staff there from rendering efficient and cheerful service; I am grateful to them and to their colleagues in the Department of Special Collections and the Kansas Collection, both housed in the Kenneth Spencer Research Library. Permission to work in the increasingly crowded British Library in London is a privilege for an American scholar, and this one certainly regards it as such.

My wife, Carol Dinsdale Worth, helped me unsnarl my more tangled prose; her vigilance as a copy editor adds one more debt to the many I owe her.

Like Tom Brown at the School-house match, Penny Parker and the staff of the Wescoe Hall Word Processing Center entered the fray at a critical moment, and gratitude is due to them as well.

Chronology

August. Contributes "The Struggle for Kansas" to Ludlow's *A Sketch of the History of the United States.*

1863 *The Cause of Freedom.* Begins contributing to the *Reader,* January.

1865 Elected M.P. for Lambeth, July. Joins the Jamaica Committee, December.

1866 Becomes chairman of the Crystal Palace Company. Becomes special London correspondent of the *New York Tribune.*

1867 Appointed to the royal commission on trade unions.

1868 Elected M.P. for Frome, Somersetshire.

1869 Becomes Queen's Counsel. Edits *The Trades' Unions of England* by the Count of Paris. *Alfred the Great.*

1870 Helps to found the Church Reform Union. First visit to North America, August-October.

1872 Becomes principal of the London Working Men's College.

1873 *Memoir of a Brother.*

1874 Appointed to the royal commission to examine the Criminal Law Amendment Act (1871), the Master and Servant Act (1867), and the law of conspiracy.

1878 *The Old Church.*

1879 *The Manliness of Christ.*

1880 Rugby settlement in Tennessee officially opened with Hughes in attendance, October 5.

1881 *Rugby, Tennessee.*

1882 *Memoir of Daniel Macmillan.* Becomes a county court judge.

1886 *Life and Times of Peter Cooper.*

1887 *James Fraser.*

1889 *David Livingstone.*

1895 *Vacation Rambles.*

1896 Dies at Brighton, Sussex, March 22.

Chapter One

A Sketch of the Life

Boyhood in Berkshire

One of the most perceptive recent writers on Thomas Hughes, Asa Briggs, said of him that "to some extent he remained a boy all his life."[1] As we shall see, there is considerable justice in this assessment of the man, and as an author Hughes drew heavily on what he called his "early memories."[2] Therefore, no reader of his novels or of his nonfictional works can afford to overlook their autobiographical elements, especially those dating back to his formative years.

The village of Uffington in the Berkshire Downs of England some sixty miles west of London was a sleepy and secluded place when Thomas Hughes was born there on October 20, 1822.[3] The closest town of any size was Wantage, seven miles away, and it could be reached only by poor roads that were almost impassable in bad weather. The most prominent landmark in Uffington was the twelfth-century parish church, whose vicar, also named Thomas Hughes, was the grandfather of the future author of *Tom Brown's School Days.*

Young Tom's roots in the village and its church were deep. His grandmother was the daughter, granddaughter, and great-granddaughter of three earlier vicars of Uffington, all named George Watts, and the Reverend Thomas Hughes had accepted the living there after his marriage to Mary Ann Watts because of her great fondness for the place. Their only child, John Hughes (1790–1857), moved into a farmhouse close to the church when he married Margaret Wilkinson in 1820, and it was here that Tom, the couple's second son, spent the first eleven years of his life.

Two miles south of Uffington, plainly visible from the children's nursery window and dominating the surrounding countryside, was—and is—White Horse Hill, so called because of the huge chalky animal figure carved out of its green side. It was still believed in the Vale of the White Horse when Hughes was growing up there that this was a monument to King Alfred's great victory over the Danes at nearby Ashdown in 871; within Hughes's lifetime, however, scholars came to the conclusion that the White Horse was actually much older than that, dating back as far as the first or second century B.C. In a ritual whose ancient origins remain obscure, it was periodically cleaned and weeded by inhabitants of the Vale—hence the title of Hughes's second novel, *The Scouring of the White Horse*—and that necessary chore was followed by communal revelry.

Near the White Horse are the vestiges of an Iron Age fort called Uffington Castle and Wayland Smith's Cave, or Wayland's Smithy, a Neolithic chamber tomb. This is approached by the prehistoric Ridgeway, which also leads to Dragon Hill, supposedly the site of St. George's slaying of the dragon. It was in this storied countryside that the boy Thomas Hughes first experienced the exhilaration of the outdoors and the challenge of games and sports, which were to remain a lifelong passion with him.

But there was a darker side to that happy time, for the early 1830s were the years of the "Swing riots," when disaffected agricultural laborers were terrorizing much of rural southern England with acts of arson and pillage. "My father was the most active magistrate in the district," Hughes wrote a half-century later, "and was constantly in the saddle, keeping the King's peace. He was an old fashioned Tory, but with true popular sympathies, and had played cricket and football all his life with the men and boys of our village, and it is one of my proudest memories that only one man from Uffington joined the rioters, and he came back after three weeks ashamed and penitent."[4] Before he was ten, the future Christian Socialist was learning about the English class system and also about the violence to which the desperation of impoverished workers might bring them and their society.

Reading was not one of this active boy's favorite pastimes; but his paternal grandmother had many literary acquaintances, and his father was himself something of an author. A formidable woman by all accounts, Mary Ann Hughes knew writers like Sir Walter Scott, Robert Southey, Thomas Hood, and Harrison Ainsworth, and Tom would often meet such celebrities when visiting his grandparents at the London home where they spent six months of each year while the Reverend Dr. Hughes performed his duties as canon of St. Paul's Cathedral. John Hughes edited the *Boscobel Tracts* (1830), a widely read account of the travels and trials of Charles Stuart after his Royalist forces lost the Battle of Worcester during the English Civil War, and published a good deal of prose and verse. As for Tom, he was fond of poetry, especially that of Scott; and, very much like other children of his class at the time, he was encouraged to read edifying books like *The Pilgrim's Progress, Robinson Crusoe,* and *The History of Sandford and Merton.*

School Days and Oxford

Hughes's formal education began at the age of eight, when he was sent to a private preparatory school at Twyford in neighboring Hampshire along with his older brother George. One feature of the Twyford curriculum that must have appealed to the athletic Tom was that it included instruction in gymnastics. It also stressed the reading and memorization of poetry, and Tom took that opportunity to learn by heart several of the longer works of his favorite writer, Scott.

The most momentous step in Hughes's education, if not his whole life, was taken when his father decided to enroll Tom and George at Rugby after they had been at Twyford a little over three years. Then as now one of the best-known English public schools, Rugby was recovering from a long period of decline because of the exertions of Dr. Thomas Arnold, the eminent churchman, historian, and—as it turned out—educational reformer, whom John Hughes had known at Oxford and who had become headmaster in 1828.

It was not primarily the course of study that Arnold revamped at Rugby: this retained the traditional emphasis on Latin and Greek, with some attention to Scripture, history, mathematics, and French.[5] Rather, he tried "to make the school far more a corporate unit than it had been," by giving more authority to the masters, or teachers, and by relying on the prepostors of the sixth form, the senior pupils, "to set the moral tone of the school."[6] Arnold was troubled by the unruliness of the boys, the bullying of the weak by the strong, and the abuses that had crept into the old system of fagging, according to which the younger pupils were supposed to run errands and do menial tasks for the sixth-formers; but he was especially anxious to make Rugby " 'a place of Christian education,' " " 'to form Christian men, for' "—boys being what they are—" 'Christian boys I can never hope to make.' "[7] His commitment to upright thought and virtuous action suffused by Christian ideals was plainly to be seen in his work as a teacher, examiner, and administrator, his social contacts with his

charges, and especially his memorable Sunday afternoon chapel sermons. By those means, he generated in many of his pupils an awe of
him that was to endure for decades after they left school.

Though never a member of the inner circle of Arnold's most fer-
vent disciples, Hughes was among those who were affected and influenced by the man and his ideas. Returning to Rugby to give a
speech near the end of his life, Hughes talked of the critical importance of "the years from ten till eighteen or nineteen," going on to
affirm that "I passed all those years under the spell of this place
and Arnold, and for half a century have never ceased to thank God
for it." Arnold had taught him and his contemporaries, he said, that
life is "a fight which would last all our lives, and try all our powers,
physical, intellectual, and moral, to the utmost. . . . the world-old one
of good with evil, of light and truth against darkness and lies, of
Christ against the devil."[8] This Arnoldian view of life as a struggle
is prominent throughout Hughes's work, beginning with *Tom Brown's
School Days.* Along with Arthur Penrhyn Stanley's *The Life and Correspondence of Thomas Arnold, D.D.* (1844) and a famous poem by
Arnold's son Matthew, "Rugby Chapel" (1867), Hughes's first novel
turned his headmaster into a legendary figure for a large reading
audience in the second half of the nineteenth century.

Though Hughes was profoundly moved by the religious, ethical,
and social precepts Arnold espoused, his advocacy of intellectual rigor
had little effect on the youngster. He did not distinguish himself in
his studies, but devoted most of his considerable energy to games and
sports, especially cricket and Rugby football, eventually becoming captain of both teams. It is not surprising, therefore, that we learn much
less about mental than about physical activity in Hughes's autobiographical reminiscences of Rugby and in *Tom Brown's School Days*
itself. When A. P. Stanley read that novel, he professed to be as-
tounded at its depiction of the rough-and-tumble side of school life.
" 'It is an absolute revelation to me: opens up a world of which,
though so near me, I was utterly ignorant.' "[9] The fact that Hughes
and Stanley, who left Rugby loaded with scholastic honors soon after
Hughes arrived there in February 1834, seemed to live in worlds apart
while attending the same school at virtually the same time tells us
much not only about the two of them, the exuberant extrovert and
the more withdrawn student, but also about Rugby as it was in the
1830s.

Hughes did not want to leave Rugby but had to when he reached nineteen, the maximum age permitted at the school. In 1842 he went up to Oxford, to Oriel, his father's old college, where Arnold had held a fellowship a quarter-century earlier. At the beginning of his university career, he paid too much attention to sports—rowing and boxing now, as well as football and cricket—so that his first year there, as he wrote later, "was utterly wasted." "The lectures were perfectly easy to me as I had read all the books at Rugby, and I employed no private tutor. . . . I happened to fall into an idle, fast set, just as did the rest, and made a fool of myself in all the usual ways."[10]

But that changed following the long vacation of 1843 when he became engaged to Frances Ford, a clergyman's daughter whom he had met the preceding winter. Her father was understandably skeptical about the seriousness and the prospects of this young couple, he barely into his twenties and she only seventeen; with the new incentive of approaching matrimony, however, Hughes settled down to his studies and took his degree less than two years later.

In other ways, whose significance he could not have appreciated at the time, Hughes spent these two years equipping himself for the life he was to lead after graduation. He became an avid reader, especially moved by one book by his old headmaster and another one about him: *Christian Life* (1841), a collection of Arnold's sermons; and Stanley's biography. Not surprisingly, Arnold's ideas were coming to weigh much more heavily with Hughes now that he was about to assume the responsibilities of adulthood than they ever had while he was a pupil at Rugby. Deeply pained by the increasing fragmentation of society and by the growing gap between rich and poor, powerful and powerless, Arnold had urged his boys to prepare themselves for the task of bringing the people of the nation together once they assumed the positions of authority to which their public-school education would entitle them.

Arnold's views were reinforced at this time in Hughes's life by those of another writer who was to have a profound influence on him: Thomas Carlyle, whose *Past and Present* (1843) he read soon after it appeared. Carlyle's vision of a demoralized and divided nation that could only be restored to health under the guidance of a wise aristocracy of talent and enlightened captains of industry, fully aware of the spiritual dimensions of their world and of their responsibilities in it, struck a responsive chord in Hughes's mind.

Other events were shaping Hughes's emerging political and social beliefs. While traveling in the north of England during the long vacation of 1844, he engaged in discussions with businessmen who favored the repeal of the Corn Laws, which kept the price of bread high and so caused much misery during the "hungry forties," and he found their arguments to be persuasive. At about the same time, he became interested in the People's Charter, a series of demands by working men that Parliament, to which they had no right to elect representatives, be made responsive to the will of all classes, including theirs. Hughes was beginning to subject the easygoing Toryism in which he had been raised to searching scrutiny and to think more and more about democracy, a suspect word in the 1840s, while recalling Arnold's and Carlyle's warnings that pure, unchecked, materialistic democracy would never work well in practice.

Starting Out in London

After giving some consideration to entering the church like his Watts forebears and the grandfather for whom he had been named, Hughes decided instead on a career in the law and began the required course of reading at Lincoln's Inn, London, in 1845. He applied himself diligently to his legal apprenticeship, and his personal and professional lives moved along swiftly together. He earned his first fee in the spring of 1846, his engagement to Fanny Ford was announced that Christmas, they were married in August 1847, and he was admitted to the bar the following January.

By then it was clear that Hughes's career as a lawyer would be no ordinary one. Several recent experiences had driven him inexorably toward what would today be called social activism; and there is something appropriate in the fact that he earned his professional credentials in the fateful year 1848, which was marked by social and political revolutions on the European Continent. In Hughes's own country, a similar upheaval appeared to be threatened. The Chartists, as the advocates of the People's Charter were called, had announced that they would hold a mass meeting on April 10 on Kennington Common, south of the Thames, to be followed by a march on the Houses of Parliament across the river. The nervous government was ready for trouble: troops were stationed all over the capital and 150,000 special constables, among whom was Thomas Hughes, were on duty. But no trouble came. The enthusiasm of the crowd, estimated at twenty thousand, was dampened by rain, and the demonstrators' way to Westminster was barred at Waterloo Bridge. As Torben Christensen had written, "the day marked the *fiasco* of Chartism."[11]

During the previous three years in London, Hughes had witnessed the kind of poverty, squalor, and exploitation that fed the fires of Chartism, and he soon came to see one way in which, true to the ideals of Arnold, he might enlist in the Christian warfare against deprivation and injustice. In 1846 he had begun attending the sermons delivered in the chapel of Lincoln's Inn by Frederick Denison Maurice, for Hughes a spellbinding preacher whom he likened to St. Paul; in the following year Hughes had written Maurice to suggest that, contrary to the rules under which worship was conducted there, a collection be taken up for the benefit of Irish people who were starving in that island's famine. In the wake of the debacle of April 10, 1848, with none of the problems that had given rise to Chartism resolved, Maurice joined with another clergyman, Charles Kingsley, and a lawyer, John Malcolm Ludlow, to found what became known as the Christian Socialist movement, and Hughes offered Maurice his services.

Maurice asked his growing band of supporters what they would think of having this new recruit join them. As Ludlow, around whose dinner table that meeting was conducted, told the story, one man objected. " 'Tom Hughes? Oh, he won't do. A very good fellow for a cricket match, or as umpire at football, but no good for teaching.' " But after Hughes was introduced to the company—"a strapping young fellow, with blue-grey eyes, fresh complexioned, with a bright open countenance and singularly sunny smile, the very type of a manly young English squire"—all opposition vanished.[12]

Ludlow's guest had spoken of teaching, and indeed the Christian Socialists always viewed education as their primary task, even before they founded the London Working Men's College, with Maurice as principal, in 1854. In their judgment, class warfare of the sort advocated by many Chartists would only exacerbate the problems of English society in an increasingly industrialized and urbanized age. What was necessary in order to relieve the misery of the modern worker was to acknowledge his individual worth, with which his Creator had endowed him; to foster his practical skills, his intellect, and his moral nature; to lead him to act in enlightened and constructive ways to further his own interests; and above all to teach him that the business of God's world must be conducted along coopera-

tive rather than competitive lines. During their relatively brief existence as a coherent movement,[13] the Christian Socialists worked toward these goals in a variety of ways: through propaganda from the
pulpit and the speaker's platform and in their publications; through
the creation of new forms of employment, beginning with the Working Tailors' Association in 1850; and through legislation that would
facilitate the establishment of such cooperative enterprises and make
them economically viable.

"I am not much of a thinker or projector," Hughes wrote with
characteristic modesty of his involvement in the Christian Socialist
movement.[14] Nevertheless, even if ideas were not his strong suit, it is
clear that by his capacity for hard work and his ability to reconcile
conflicting points of view he contributed at least as much as its other
leaders. Indeed, he probably did more than anyone else to hold together the diverse and often difficult personalities who had hoisted the
banner of Christian Socialism, and he was instrumental in drawing in
a number of other figures whose allegiance it was important to secure.
Hughes was a tireless speaker and an effective organizer. He helped
bring about the Industrial and Provident Societies Act of 1852, which
gave important legal rights to cooperative associations. He raised
money for the movement and donated a considerable amount of his
own. After the Working Men's College was established, he taught
boxing there, organized its cricket and rowing clubs, presided over its
social evenings, and served as major-commandant of its volunteer
corps during the French invasion scare of 1859—all with infectious
enthusiasm.

Hughes also aided the Christian Socialist cause with his pen. He
had not, as far as we know, done much writing for publication before
affiliating himself with the movement, though a poem of his had
appeared in *Ainsworth's Magazine* while he was still an undergraduate.[15] The fame that *Tom Brown's School Days* was to bring him was
still some years away. But in the early 1850s he learned that writing
would give him an excellent chance to expound arguments that he
believed to be of great importance, and he seized that chance whenever he could.

Hughes had not yet joined the Christian Socialists when the first of
their three penny weeklies, *Politics for the People,* ran its brief course
between May and July 1848; but he contributed to the second, the
Christian Socialist, in 1850–51, and edited its successor, the *Journal
of Association*, during the first four months of 1852. When it expired

a few weeks later, Maurice for one was not sorry; the spiritual leader of the movement, whom his associates revered as their "Prophet," never had much faith in periodical journalism, preferring that they commit their message to a series of "Tracts on Christian Socialism." Maurice himself had led off with a *Dialogue between Somebody (a Person of Respectability) and Nobody (the Writer)*; Hughes followed with his much more down-to-earth *History of the Working Tailors' Association* (1850). In addition to explaining how the first cooperative venture in London had come into being, the *History* also served as a Christian Socialist manifesto and a concise statement of Hughes's beliefs. "The sign of the Cross is the one under which we shall still conquer," he wrote, "the only one which will give brotherhood a victory over competition, love over hatred, truth over falsehood" (*History*, 10).

Other such pieces followed—short, hard-hitting, polemical. In 1852 Hughes published *A Lecture on the Slop-System* he had delivered at the Reading Literary and Mechanics' Institution; this gave a graphic description of the degradation to which the evils of competition had reduced the needlewomen of London. *King's College and Mr. Maurice* (1854) protested the dismissal of the "Prophet" from the two professorial chairs he had held at that institution. Though not published until 1860, Hughes's *Account of the Lock-Out of Engineers* dealt with the birth-struggle of the first modern trade union in England, the Amalgamated Society of Engineers, in 1851–52. (Hughes and his colleagues in the Society for Promoting Working Men's Associations had watched this with great interest, lending whatever help they could.) None of these writings possesses any literary value, but they do show Hughes's eagerness to set his convictions down in print, as he was later to do in his more durable works.

Throughout the period of his energetic efforts on behalf of Christian Socialism, Hughes was also establishing himself as a lawyer and a family man. Maurice, the first of his children (there were to be nine in all), was eight years old in the summer of 1856 when Hughes, "thinking over what I should like to say to him before he went to school," "took to writing a story, as the easiest way of bringing out what I wanted."[16] The result was *Tom Brown's School Days* (1857), the first and by all odds the most famous of the three novels he wrote in quick succession. *The Scouring of the White Horse*, set in the Berkshire countryside where he had grown up, followed late the next year; and the story of his first, somewhat autobiographical, protagonist was carried down through his university career in *Tom Brown at Oxford* (1861). Though Hughes lived for thirty-five more years and never stopped writing, he published only one more piece of short fiction: "The Ashen Faggot" (1862), a Christmas story about the return of a prodigal son to his West Country home.[17]

The Public Man

A new phase in Hughes's life began on July 12, 1865, when he was elected to represent the largely working-class London constituency of Lambeth in the House of Commons, where he remained for nine years. In the 1868 general election he contested and won the seat for the rural Somerset town of Frome rather than that for Lambeth, from whose voters he had come to feel increasingly estranged. Many of them kept small shops or public houses, and they did not appreciate Hughes's support of legislation against the sale of adulterated goods and Sunday trading or in favor of honest weights and measures and strict licensing hours for drinking establishments.

Being the man he was, Hughes was bound to use his position as a Member of Parliament to promote his religious, moral, and social beliefs and his vision of a nation in which greed and misery would be abolished when Christian cooperation became a reality rather than to serve the short-term interests of his constituents. His maiden speech, ostensibly on the subject of the 1866 Reform Bill, was really a plea for improving the lot of the suffering working class,[18] a theme he continued to urge during his whole parliamentary career. Among the legislation he sponsored were bills to strengthen the position of cooperative societies and trade unions, to require railway companies to provide new housing for city dwellers displaced by the building of new lines, to bring about a fifty-four-hour week, and to improve the still scandalously poor state of urban sanitation.

Though Hughes was not a notably effective speaker or persuasive politician in the House, more often than not turning out to be on the losing side in his parliamentary battles, he was widely respected. In his *British Senators: Or, Political Sketches, Past and Present*, J. Ewing Ritchie praised Hughes as "a model of what a working man M.P. should be; firm in principle, conciliatory in utterance, ready to express his convictions and to carry them whether they are popular or the reverse" and provided an amusing glimpse of his rather unorthodox following, saying that he "seems to have many acquaintances of an humbler position in society than that to which he himself evidently belongs. All the out-of-door agitators who get up the steam, or at any rate who think they do, in the metropolis, are familiar with him; and you see him shaking hands with deputations clearly of an industrial origin, and representing co-operative societies or trades unions."[19]

From the mid-1860s on, Hughes was also deeply involved in other public activities. He was a member of the Reform League, which worked for a further extension of the franchise. He served on two royal commissions that were charged with investigating the state of the law regarding trade unions. Together with John Stuart Mill, Charles Darwin, and Thomas Henry Huxley, he was a leading figure on the Jamaica Committee, which sought to bring to justice the governor of that West Indian colony, Edward Eyre, for his ruthless suppression of a native uprising in 1865. In 1866 he became chairman of the Crystal Palace Company; and in 1872, following F. D. Maurice's death, he succeeded him as principal of the Working Men's College.

Meanwhile, Hughes continued his exertions on behalf of the rapidly growing cooperative movement. He presided at cooperative congresses, he was instrumental in founding several new cooperative enterprises, and he wrote and spoke at every opportunity about the mission of cooperation as he conceived of it: to end, rather than to intensify, the class struggle; and to achieve moral and spiritual, rather than merely material, goals for working men and women. For example, in his *Lecture on the History & Objects of Co-operation* (Manchester, 1878), he emphasized the Christian basis of the movement and its high aspirations. "The very thought of a nation whose industry is organised on co-operative principles fills the mind with visions of a time when the love of work, when pride in the work of the hands, as well as the brain, will take its place again ... in the lives of our people—when at last the great problem of the nineteenth century will be solved, and the union between labour and capital will stand out as a fact, and not as a dream" (*Lecture*, 27). In the preface he wrote three years later to the *Manual for Co-operators*—the work of Edward Vansittart Neale, though Hughes is listed on the title page as coeditor—he felt compelled to stress the differences between cooperation and other working-class movements such as communism and to reaffirm its religious dimension, its insistence "that we must be fellow-workers and not rivals, brethren of one family to whom indeed the great inheritance of this earth has been given, but only on the condition that it shall be used and enjoyed in the spirit and according to the will of Him who created it" (*Manual*, xiv).

Hughes spoke on other subjects as well during these years, as we shall see, and he published extensively: not only the books to be discussed in chapters 3, 4, and 5, but also travel pieces in the *Spectator* (collected in *Vacation Rambles* [1895]), articles in *Macmillan's Magazine* and other periodicals, and London dispatches in the *New York Tribune*.

The American Connection

Busy as he was at home, Hughes also paid close attention to events three thousand miles away in North America. As early as 1850, he was "more interested in the United States slavery question than in any political topic of that particular time in England,"[20] and he was overwhelmed by the discovery that the poetry of James Russell Lowell, to which J. M. Ludlow introduced him just then, gave vivid expression to his own loathing of slavery, an institution that he never ceased to regard as an abomination in the sight of God. In 1859 Hughes contributed a preface to the first English edition of Lowell's *The Biglow Papers*; even earlier, he had begun what was to become a lifelong habit of quoting the American poet at every opportunity.[21]

Hughes did not meet Lowell until his first American trip in 1870, though they began corresponding in the 1850s. He did, however, associate with a number of other Americans who came to England before and during the Civil War to make the Northern case. By introducing such pro-Union men as Henry Adams and Moncure Conway to his wide circle of influential friends, Hughes helped them spread their views in important quarters.[22] Hughes himself spoke out so frequently in support of the Northern position that the American abolitionist William Lloyd Garrison later hailed him for having stood among "those on this side of the Atlantic who, in the midst of our terrible struggle, were able to understand its nature, and to give a clear and unequivocal testimony on behalf of the right."[23]

The course Hughes had chosen in siding publicly with the Union was not an easy one to follow in the England of the early 1860s. For a variety of reasons, the aristocracy and the commercial classes, which still wielded great power, favored the Confederacy. So did such important daily and weekly papers as the *Times* and the *Saturday*

Review. Even the working class, which was generally sympathetic to the Union, was injured by the Northern duties on foreign goods and by the interruption of the supply of Southern cotton to English textile mills. Early in the war, the so-called *Trent* affair blemished the Northern image and nearly led to armed conflict between Britain and the Union.[24]

But it was characteristic of Hughes to take unpopular positions and say what he believed rather than what his audiences wanted to hear. He behaved the same way when he visited North America for the first time at Lowell's invitation in the summer and fall of 1870, five years after Appomattox. On his travels through the United States, which took him as far west as Omaha, Hughes told anyone who would listen why England had maintained her neutrality during the great American conflict.

Hughes was fascinated by what he saw of the United States and Canada on this trip, especially by the possibilities that their vast stretches of undeveloped land might hold out to citizens of his own increasingly crowded country. Ten years later, convinced that English society had changed in ways that were making it impossible for the nation to go on absorbing the products of the public schools and that emigration would do much to ameliorate this and other social problems, Hughes founded the cooperative settlement of Rugby in Tennessee. Though launched amid high hopes in 1880, this colony soon collapsed as the result of a series of misfortunes: bad weather, disease, the lackadaisical work habits of the English settlers, and the rascality of the American speculators who had sold them land—not very good land, as it turned out, and in many cases land whose title was in dispute.

We shall examine the literary fruit that Hughes's absorption with America bore in chapter 4.

The Later Years in Chester

Among the consequences of the Rugby disaster was Hughes's financial ruin. He estimated his loss as at least £7,000, a considerable fortune at that time, and was forced to give up his house and his legal practice in London, accepting an appointment as a county judge so that he might earn more money and spend less. In order to be near his circuit, Hughes and his wife moved to the walled cathedral city of Chester, where they had a house built in 1885. Recalling the Berkshire village where Hughes had been born sixty-three years earlier, they named it Uffington House.[25]

Under blows that would have flattened lesser men—bitter disappointment, bereavement, illness, and the unmistakable onset of old age—Hughes remained active and in good spirits in this new setting. While carrying on his judicial work, he kept up his interest in public affairs, continuing to speak out on church, cooperative, and educational questions. He hailed the founding of the Christian Social Union by several Anglican clergymen in 1889, regarding it as a welcome successor of the Christian Socialist movement in which he had played such a large role in an earlier generation, and he contributed reminiscences of Maurice and Neale to its magazine, the *Economic Review*. He made his last crossing to the United States in 1887, but he went on traveling in England, France, and Italy and setting down his impressions for the *Spectator* until nearly the end of his life. In addition to such periodical articles and the biographies of Daniel Macmillan, Peter Cooper, James Fraser, and David Livingstone that will be treated in chapter 5, his publications during these final years included the texts of several speeches in which he continued to assert his long-cherished principles while lamenting the growing materialism and contentiousness into which he saw his country slipping as the century drew toward its close.

Hughes died unexpectedly on March 22, 1896, at the south coast port of Brighton while en route to Italy once more. By then he was revered throughout the English-speaking world, and a writer in the *Spectator* no doubt spoke for many when he declared that Hughes's passing "will probably have caused a more diffused and general feeling of personal grief than would have been caused by any other death that could have taken place."[26]

Chapter Two

The Novels

Though the work by which he is best known, *Tom Brown's School Days* (1857), is a novel, Thomas Hughes never thought of himself as a novelist. Nonetheless, *Tom Brown's School Days* and also its two successors in that form, *The Scouring of the White Horse* (1858) and *Tom Brown at Oxford* (1861), remain of interest for several reasons. Written in his thirties, after the disintegration of the Christian Socialist movement, they express Hughes's continuing engagement with the issues that had brought him into the company of such men as Maurice, Kingsley, Ludlow, and Neale. They look back even farther, nostalgically but not uncritically, to Hughes's boyhood in Berkshire and at school and to his years at Oxford University; but they also anticipate his future concern with those questions of church and state that were to occupy him during the rest of his long career as a public figure.

Above all, despite their imperfections, Hughes's three novels are still remarkably readable as fiction, especially if they are approached with some sense of the context in which they first appeared.

Tom Brown's School Days

Tom Brown, the eldest son of a Berkshire squire, attends Rugby School from the time he is ten until he is nineteen years old. He does not actually get to Rugby until the fifth chapter of the novel; and, though what happens to him there is clearly Hughes's chief concern, it is impossible to understand Tom's public-school career without giving some attention to his background and early life.

In the opening chapter of *Tom Brown's School Days* Hughes goes to considerable lengths to show that his protagonist has sprung from sturdy English stock. The members of the far-flung Brown family are uncomplicated, straightforward, honest, and honorable people; they doggedly defend what is right and attack what is wrong; they stick together; and they are not easily daunted or discouraged. By their strength, their courage, their persistence, and their keen if not always broad or deep vision, they, along with other families like theirs, have made the nation and the British Empire what they are.

The fact that he belongs to such a family endows Tom with a formidable heritage. The further fact that his particular branch of the Browns occupies a prominent position in the county of Berkshire is also of great significance. As squire and justice of the peace, Tom's father is looked up to by the entire village, and Tom's mother is known and loved for her good works among the sick. Though he is a staunch Tory, Squire Brown does not hold himself aloof from the lower classes or teach his children to do so; on the contrary, he firmly believes "that a man is to be valued wholly and solely for that which he is in himself . . . apart from clothes, rank, fortune, and all externals whatsoever."[1]

These Browns, like Hughes's own family, live in the Vale of the White Horse, and much of the first chapter is given over to a lyrical and highly detailed account of the beauties and the historical and legendary associations of that neighborhood. Beginning in early childhood, Tom Brown acquires an intimate and loving knowledge of these few square miles of Berkshire, and Hughes insists that this sort of close association with one's birthplace, one's roots, which cheap and rapid railway transportation has rendered virtually obsolete by the time his novel is published, makes for a fundamental stability of character.

In anticipation of a theme that is to become dominant when Tom is a pupil at Rugby, we see him even during these first years constantly attempting to assert his independence. It is not a question, now or later, of doing without guidance so much as it is a question of finding the right sort of guidance for a free-spirited youngster. By the time he is four years old, Tom has broken away from the tutelage of his nurse and comes under the influence of Benjy, a seventy-year-old retired servant of the family who is full of entrancing stories about the Browns and the Vale of the White Horse and who initiates young Tom into the mysteries of fishing.

One of the highlights of this association occurs when Benjy takes Tom to the annual "veast" commemorating the dedication of the parish church. In addition to providing more White Horse Vale local color, this scene, which takes up most of I, 2, makes two points that are to have great significance later in *Tom Brown's School Days* and Hughes's other novels.

First, we are introduced to the sport of backswording, a great attraction at such festivals. It is the object of this traditional Berkshire diversion to open a bleeding wound in the head of one's opponent with a cudgel, which requires only a slight blow of that weapon. The important thing is to play by the rules so as to test and demonstrate one's skill rather than to inflict injury or pain.

Second, Hughes emphasizes in one of his countless asides that, a generation and more before he writes, "feast-time was the day of reconciliation for the parish" (*School Days*, I, 2; 34), when not only people of different persuasions but also members of all classes came together in amity. That this is no longer the spirit that informs such events, that they have degenerated into the sort of depraved spectacle that Hughes's friend Kingsley described in chapter 13 of his novel *Yeast* (1851), is an ominous sign of the way society at mid-century has become increasingly fragmented.

After Benjy's rheumatism puts an end to his outings with the boy, Tom associates increasingly with village lads his own age, roaming the countryside and engaging in strenuous sports and games in their company. It disturbs neither Tom nor his father that his new friends are the social inferiors of the squire's son: "equality or inequality" is no issue, "except in wrestling, running, and climbing" (*School Days*, I, 3; 62).

Tom's year at the private school he attends before going to Rugby is important chiefly in the way that its shortcomings point up the virtues of the much larger public school. The system there is not all bad any more than that at Rugby is all good, but it subjects the boys to constant supervision by poorly educated teachers rather than leaving them at times to their own resources; it encourages tale-bearing, which is frowned on at Rugby; and it breeds a tyranny of the strong over the weak that is much more blatant than the bullying that goes on at Arnold's school. When an outbreak of fever closes the place down, Tom is not sorry.

Why Tom wants to go on to Rugby is not at all obvious, though such a public school is normally the next step in the education of a boy of his class—and, besides, he is convinced that anything would be better than the inferior and excessively restrictive private school he has been attending. Why Squire Brown wants to send Tom to Rugby is much clearer: not in order to give him a sound classical education or to allow him to rub elbows with the future leaders of the nation, but rather to turn him into "a brave, helpful, truth-telling

Englishman, and a gentleman, and Christian" (*School Days*, I, 4; 74).

It is the development of Tom's character rather than of his intellect at Rugby that also interests Hughes. Obviously unable to depict everything that happens to his young protagonist over a span of nearly nine years there, the novelist singles out for special treatment those crucial episodes during which Tom either adapts himself to the practices of the school or else rebels against them, in either case absorbing lessons that have little or nothing to do with the formal course of study.

This learning process begins as soon as Tom arrives: of the thirteen chapters of *Tom Brown's School Days* devoted to Tom's career at Rugby, two describe in some detail his first day at school. These two chapters provide an essential introduction to the physical appearance of Rugby School as it was in the early 1830s; more significantly, they also show Tom surviving an extended initiation that sets the stage for much that is to befall him later.

Tom's guide through that eventful first day is an exuberant fellow pupil by the name of Harry East, who will become one of Tom's best friends at Rugby and a kind of barometer of the growth and change that he undergoes there. In addition to showing Tom around, East also serves him as a social arbiter. Almost as soon as he catches his first glimpse of Tom, for example, East is shocked by the fact that he is wearing a cap rather than a hat. " 'Only the louts wear caps' " (*School Days*, I, 5; 87), East says scornfully, using the derisive term by which the schoolboys refer to the town boys, and immediately takes Tom to a hatter's shop so that he may buy the only form of head covering acceptable at Rugby. He purchases this "regulation cat-skin" on credit, discovering in the process "his new social position and dignities" (*School Days*, I, 5; 88).

It so happens that this particular November Saturday is the occasion of the "School-house match," a football contest between the house where both Tom and East board and the rest of the school. To the modern American reader, this match seems chaotic in the extreme: the sport in question, of course, is Rugby football, and—rather than numbering fifteen players, as in the modern version—each team comprises as many boys as are able and willing to take part. Always eager to perform feats of physical skill, Tom, new boy though he is, unhesitatingly joins the School-house side and distinguishes himself in a key play, getting the wind knocked out of him in the process and earning the respect of Old Brooke, head of the team, who says approvingly that Tom " 'is a plucky youngster, and will make a player' " (*School Days*, I, 5; 109).

Time is called at five o'clock, and the match is to be resumed the following Saturday. But even though the result is not yet final, it is clear that the fifty or sixty School-house boys have done very well against an opposing team more than twice as numerous. The School-house side is better organized and better drilled; or, as Old Brooke says in a victory celebration that evening: "we've more reliance on one another, more of a house feeling, more fellowship than the School can have. Each of us knows and can depend on his next-hand man better—that's why we beat 'em to-day. We've union, they've division—there's the secret' " (*School Days*, I, 6; 117).

These remarks of Old Brooke's are delivered at a "singing," an event that is held in the School-house hall on each of the last six Saturdays of the first term. While he has the floor, Old Brooke, who will be leaving Rugby at the end of the half-year, cautions his juniors about the evils of bullying and drinking that still plague the house, and launches into an eloquent defense of Dr. Arnold, who has been trying, in the face of resistance from those boys who favor the traditional anarchy, to put a stop to such abuses. Arnold himself has already made one appearance on Tom's first day at Rugby, watching the School-house match with his family. Tom sees him again later that evening, a remote, awe-inspiring figure who presides at prayers with "that deep, ringing, searching voice of his" (*School Days*, I, 6; 123).

But Tom's first-day initiation is not yet over. As a new arrival, he is required to participate in the singing by standing on a table and performing a solo. His expert rendition of an old West Country song meets with general approval, and so he is spared the punishment meted out to those who fail to meet this challenge: having to down a large mug of salt water. And, finally, he is dragged out of bed by a group of fifth-formers, led by the school bully, Flashman, and subjected to the ritual of blanket-tossing, during which the victim is catapulted toward the ceiling from a blanket that is pulled taut by his tormentors while he is lying on it. Following East's advice, Tom does not struggle or go rigid, taking "his three tosses without a kick or a cry, and was called a young trump for his pains" (*School Days*, I, 6; 126).

The rest of Tom's first half-year at Rugby receives much more cursory treatment than this richly instructive and generally quite successful first day. He is placed in the third form, where "he found the work very easy, as he had been well grounded and knew his grammar by heart" (*School Days*, I, 7; 133); no more than that is said about the academic side of the term. Tom is happy in School-house, which is well governed by Warner, the head of the house, and Old Brooke: there are abuses, such as bullying, but these are generally kept in check, and Tom actually rather enjoys the required fagging.

Tom's greatest enthusiasm is for games and sports, in which he takes part with characteristic energy. His involvement in a game of hare and hounds, however, leads to his first individual encounter with Dr. Arnold: because he returns late from his chase across the country-side, he is ordered to report to the headmaster's study. In contrast to some later interviews Tom has with the Doctor, this one is quite friendly. He finds Arnold in a cheerful domestic setting, building a model boat with his children, and is dismissed with the mildest of warnings.

Because he is chaplain as well as headmaster, Arnold delivers the Sunday afternoon chapel sermon each week; and, even though Tom is not especially religious, he is profoundly impressed by the Doctor's preaching, which vividly brings home to him that human life is "no fool's or sluggard's paradise into which he had wandered by chance, but a battle-field ordained from of old, where there are no spectators, but the youngest must take his side, and the stakes are life and death." Not only "by every word he spoke in his pulpit," but also "by his whole daily life," Arnold demonstrates "how that battle was to be fought; and stood there before them their fellow-soldier and the captain of their band" (*School Days*, I, 7; 132).

During Tom's second half-year, his career at Rugby takes an alarming turn for the worse. His troubles begin when he is promoted to the lower fourth form, a large and virtually unmanageable group that includes all kinds of boys from young geniuses of nine or ten to dullards well into their teens. The lack of effective discipline and the abundance of temptation to misbehave cause Tom to go astray time and again.

It is not only in the classroom that misrule prevails. After the departure of Old Brooke, Warner, and several other highly respected sixth-formers, the quality of the School-house leadership declines distressingly. The prepostors who remain are too weak to govern effectively or to prevent the victimization of the younger pupils, and a number of fifth-formers, including the odious Flashman, move into this power vacuum, asserting authority that they have no right to assume.

Being forced to fag for these fifth-formers, contrary to rule and custom, is particularly galling to the lower-school boys, and Tom leads a rebellion against the practice. This revolt brings him and his ally East into frequent conflict with Flashman. Though they ultimately prevail in what Hughes clearly intends us to view as their just cause, and though Flashman is finally expelled in disgrace for drunkenness, Tom emerges from this struggle with a damaged reputation.

Nor do Tom's animal spirits abate during this second term. On several occasions, he is summoned into the Doctor's no longer kindly presence for disciplinary action as a consequence of unacceptable behavior of one kind or another: poaching; climbing the school tower and sabotaging the great clock; going into town, against orders, during fair time. At the end of the half-year, Arnold warns Tom and his accomplice East that they face dismissal if they persist in their disorderly ways. They must understand, he tells them, that the rules at Rugby " 'are made for the good of the whole School, and must and shall be obeyed' " (*School Days*, I, 11; 187).

Having consulted the young master of their form, Arnold devises a plan to give Tom some responsibility and remove East from Tom's increasingly dangerous influence. At the beginning of the next term, Tom is asked to look after a new boy at school, the frail George Arthur. When the matron breaks the news of this scheme to Tom, his emotions are mixed: on the one hand, he is pleased to get a larger study, which he will share with Arthur; on the other hand, Tom recognizes with some dismay that this new arrangement is bound to affect his cherished intimacy with East. And what is Tom to do with his delicate charge, who sounds like the kind of milksop on whom the other boys are sure to heap ridicule? Arnold and his wife try a little flattery on the reluctant Tom, and it works: they invite him to tea to meet Arthur, "just as if he were a sixth or fifth-form boy, and of importance in the school world, instead of the most reckless young scapegrace among the fags" (*School Days*, II, 1; 193).

That Tom's agreeing to take Arthur under his wing is indeed "the turning-point in our hero's school career" (*School Days*, II, 1; 190) becomes apparent during Arthur's first evening in the dormitory. When he kneels by his bedside to pray, he draws the abuse of several of the other boys, one of whom throws a slipper at him.[2] Not only does Tom come to Arthur's defense, but he also remembers with shame a promise he made his mother "never to forget to kneel by his bedside, and give himself up to his Father, before he laid his head to rest on the pillow, from which it might never rise" (*School Days*, II, 1; 201). Tom's realization that this unworldly weakling has the courage of his convictions, whereas he himself has been too fearful of rough treatment to keep his vow, reduces him to tears. The Doctor's plan is working better than he could have hoped: Tom's moral regeneration has already begun.

And not only Tom's. The next morning, still somewhat embarrassed, Tom kneels down to pray, and as he rises to his feet he notices that "two other boys besides Arthur had already followed his example"; within a few days, "all the other boys but three or four followed the lead." Arthur's example teaches Tom, and ultimately the rest of the dormitory, "the lesson that he who has conquered his own coward spirit has conquered the whole outward world" (*School Days*, II, 1; 202).

Following this initial crisis and its fortunate outcome, Tom is scrupulous in meeting his obligations to George Arthur. Not only does he introduce him to the customs of Rugby School much as Harry East had done Tom a similar service at the time of his own arrival, but he also encourages the bookish Arthur to engage in various forms of outdoor exercise, thereby helping him to build up his weak constitution. There is more involved in this relationship than Tom's obedience to a developing sense of duty: he derives genuine satisfaction from his role as Arthur's mentor, feeling "the value of having an object in his life, something that drew him out of himself," and as a result of discharging this responsibility he is "happier than he had ever yet been at school, which was saying a great deal" (*School Days*, II, 2; 208).

From the beginning, of course, Arthur has taught Tom as much by precept and example as Tom has taught him, and this other kind of mentorship continues. The two boys take to reading the Bible together, and Arthur's interpretations of Scripture show Tom how vital and how applicable to modern conditions religious faith can be. At a level that speaks more directly to a nature like Tom's, these discussions with Arthur reinforce the momentous spiritual lessons of Dr. Arnold's sermons in Rugby Chapel.

The first time Tom sees Arthur reading his Bible, he notices that his protégé is in tears. As Tom discovers, Arthur is thinking of his father, with whom he used to study the Bible prior to his death a year earlier, and further questioning reveals that the elder Arthur was a Christian Socialist long before the term was coined—a clergyman who ministered diligently to the poor working-class people of a town in the Midlands, not only sympathizing with their misery but actually sharing it. He contracted typhus because he refused to flee the epidemic that was ravaging his parish, and he was so beloved that even the local freethinkers shared the community's grief when he succumbed to the disease.

Tom and Arthur also do their school lessons together. One kind of assignment over which they labor is called a "vulgus," succinctly defined by Hughes as "a short exercise in Greek or Latin verse, on a given subject" (*School Days*, II, 3; 225). Because the number of topics that could reasonably be set was limited, even the most ingenious teacher would sooner or later begin repeating himself, assigning subjects that he had used before; and so there arose the practice of keeping "vulgus-books," copies of such exercises that were handed on from pupil to pupil and from year to year.

Not surprisingly, Tom and Arthur differ in their attitudes toward the vulgus. Tom makes free use of vulgus-books in writing out his exercises, with no idea that he is doing anything wrong: this "traditionary method of vulgus-doing" (*School Days*, II, 3; 226), after all, is one accepted way for Rugby boys to wage the battle of wits in which they are perpetually engaged with their masters. Arthur, on the other hand, regards the vulgus as a challenge to his linguistic and creative powers, striving to turn each exercise into a polished poetic performance.

A sure sign of Arthur's growing influence over Tom is that, after Arthur has been at Rugby for two years, he finally persuades Tom to give up using vulgus-books and other schoolboy cribs. Tom protests at first. How will he get along without them? Besides, doesn't everybody resort to such aids? Such feeble arguments will not do. Arthur insists that Tom knows as well as he does that what he has been doing is wrong and that the Doctor, whom Tom claims he wants to please, would be deeply offended if he knew Tom had been guilty of plagiarism.

This successful attempt of Arthur's to bring about a new kind of honesty in Tom occurs at a period when he is particularly susceptible to Arthur's urgings. There has been an outbreak of fever at Rugby during which one boy, Thompson, has died, and several others, including Arthur, have been dangerously ill. Tom's relief at Arthur's recovery is so great that he is prepared to grant him any request; and, in addition, Tom has been profoundly moved by Arnold's chapel sermon the day after Thompson's death. At such solemn moments, the Doctor said, one's " 'eyes are opened really to know good and evil' " (*School Days*, II, 6; 263). Tom is no exception to this general rule, especially when it has been laid down in words as eloquent as Arnold's.

What Arthur has to say about his illness has other beneficial effects on Tom. Arthur's account of Dr. Arnold's spiritual ministrations as he lay near death shows Tom yet another side of his headmaster and further deepens the reverence in which he holds him, and Arthur's story of his vision of the afterlife—" 'I know it wasn't a dream' " (*School Days*, II, 6; 272), he says—reinforces the notion, which Tom has already heard from both Arthur and the Doctor, that God's work is to be done in this world as well as in the next.

That Tom has profited from Arthur's teaching is best seen in the effect that he subsequently has on his own Rugby mentor, Harry East. East is still the sort of free spirit that Tom had been; like Tom, too, he is open to good influences if these are brought to bear on him in the right way. After great effort, Tom induces East to make less use of vulgus-books and cribs. On hearing that East does not take communion because he has never been confirmed, Tom urges him to go to Dr. Arnold, make a clean breast of his religious confusion, and take the Doctor's spiritual advice. East does what Tom suggests and is much comforted by the Doctor.

Our last glimpse of Tom Brown at Rugby occurs two years later, at the end of his final year. He is now a nineteen-year-old prepostor; captain of the cricket team, which acquits itself handsomely against the professionals of the Marylebone Cricket Club; and, following Arnold's departure for his summer home in the Lake District, effectively in charge of the school. This former rebel and scapegrace has obviously grown into a responsible and successful young man.

Tom is aware that he owes that growth primarily to Arnold and George Arthur, but he does not know until his fourth-form master tells him, now at the end of his schooldays, just what Arnold had in mind in asking Tom to take charge of Arthur when Tom's fortunes at Rugby had sunk to their lowest point. The master's disclosure comes as a complete revelation to Tom: understanding at last that he has not really made his own way to the top, but that he has been following a plan devised for him by a headmaster of exceptional wisdom, Tom loses what is left of his boyish conceit, and his admiration for the Doctor rises still further. At his departure from Rugby, in fact, Tom's attitude toward Arnold is that of "a hero-worshipper, who would have satisfied the soul of Thomas Carlyle himself" (*School Days*, II, 8; 310).

The final chapter of *Tom Brown's School Days* is a kind of coda. A year out of school, Tom interrupts a fishing trip to return to Rugby after he hears of Arnold's unexpected death. Tom's grief on visiting Arnold's grave in Rugby Chapel begins as a personal, indeed a selfish, sense of loss; in keeping with what he learned at the Doctor's school and from the Doctor himself, however, his emotions soon change so that he feels "the drawing of the bond which links all living souls together in one brotherhood—at the grave beneath the altar of him who had opened his eyes to see that glory, and softened his heart till it could feel that bond." The brotherhood of man, of course, implies the fatherhood of God, and it is on this note that the novel closes: "For it is only through our mysterious human relationships . . . that we can come to the knowledge of Him in whom alone the love, and the tenderness, and the purity, and the strength, and the courage, and the wisdom of all these dwell for ever and ever in perfect fulness" (*School Days*, II, 9; 322).

Though *Tom Brown's School Days* can be read as an account of the taming, the civilizing, and the Christianizing of its young protagonist, that is not, of course, the only way to regard Hughes's novel. Its initial success owed less to its status as a *Bildungsroman*, a novel of character formation, than to its colorful portrayal of public-school life from the vantage point of a perpetual boy, Hughes himself; and its enduring appeal, even after a century and a quarter of convulsive social change, stems primarily from what one early reviewer called its "exact picture of the bright side of a Rugby boy's experiences told with a life, a spirit, and a fond minuteness of detail and recollection."[3] Historians of the novel have generally agreed with the assessment of Hughes's biographers that in writing *Tom Brown's School Days* he created a new form, the public-school novel. "His was literally the first work of fiction to present a real world of boys in the setting of a real English public school. And it is still, despite the many recent novels on the subject, the most vigorous, the most convincing, and the most deeply moving of all."[4]

There have, however, been those who have argued that Hughes's picture of Rugby life is misleading, perhaps even dangerous. Among them was Matthew Arnold, who complained that *Tom Brown's School Days* "gives the reader the impression that it is the chief business of a public school to produce a healthy animal, to supply him with pleasant companions and faithful friends, to foster in him courage and truthfulness, and for the rest to teach as much as the regulations enforce, but no more."[5] This impression led many to think of this kind of institution as a social and athletic establishment rather than as an intellectual one, a view that would have horrified Matthew Arnold's father.

Certainly there is support for such a view in the novel. We have already seen what Squire Brown's motives in sending Tom to Rugby were. As to Tom himself, when Arthur asks him what he hopes to achieve at the school, Tom's reply indicates that he does not give high priority to intellectual accomplishments: " 'I want to be A 1 at cricket and football, and all the other games, and to make my hands keep my head against any fellow, lout or gentleman. I want to get into the sixth before I leave, and to please the Doctor; and I want to carry away just as much Latin and Greek as will take me through Oxford respectably. . . . I want to leave behind me . . . the name of a fellow who never bullied a little boy, or turned his back on a big one' " (*School Days*, II, 6; 268). But, though it may be true that, as David Newsome has written, "Tom Brown was not the product which Arnold hoped to give to the world by virtue of what he preached and taught at Rugby,"[6] surely it is also arguable that in an England teeming with Tom Browns Dr. Arnold's school was able to do them, and therefore the nation, some genuine good.

Hughes's novel shows that there is a place for the introspective and studious George Arthur at Rugby, just as there is for the boisterous and athletic Tom Brown. Each boy attains an important kind of growth there, learning from the other as well as from the school curriculum. The real misfit is a young scientific enthusiast bearing the telling nickname "Madman" Martin, who keeps animals and conducts chemical experiments in his study, "with the most wondrous results in the shape of explosions and smells that mortal boy ever heard of." Hughes himself calls the Madman "one of those unfortunates who were . . . quite out of their places at a public school" (*School Days*, II, 3; 219), but we may well wonder if, after decades of so-called progressive education, there exists a school even today where such an original would get on any better than Martin did at the Rugby of *Tom Brown's School Days.*

The assertion that Hughes's depiction of Rugby life helped to bring about a weakening of the intellectual fiber of the mid- and late-nineteenth-century English public school is closely linked with another charge: that *Tom Brown's School Days* glorified a mindless sort of bodily strength, a point that was made, without any condemnation, by some of the first reviewers. One commented on the prominence of "the true Saxon delight in exercise, combat, and every manifestation of physical strength" in the novel,[7] and another applied to it the label "muscular Christianity," which had been associated with the fiction of Charles Kingsley.[8] More recent critics have deplored the excessive "pugnacity" they see in *Tom Brown's School Days.*[9]

This objection, too, grows naturally enough out of what Hughes put into his book: not only his accounts of the physical exploits of Tom and his friends, but especially his little sermons in praise of fighting. The latter, however, need to be examined with some care if they are to yield an accurate understanding of what Hughes had in mind.

In II, 5, when George Arthur is picked on by "Slogger" Williams, one of the duller and more brutish boys in their class, Tom comes to his friend's defense, battling the bully to a draw in a free-form contest that combines bare-knuckle boxing with West Country wrestling, before the Doctor's arrival on the scene puts a stop to the proceedings. Far from being a common occurrence, however, this is in fact "Tom's only single combat with a school-fellow"; "it was not at all usual in those days for two School-house boys to have a fight" (*School Days*, II, 5; 242).

Before the battle begins, Hughes makes a statement that hostile critics have held against him. "From the cradle to the grave," he says, "fighting, rightly understood, is the business, the real highest, honestest business of every son of man." But his very next sentence makes it clear that according to his definition "fighting" means far more than fisticuffs, taking in as well moral combat of the sort advocated by Arnold. "Every one who is worth his salt has his enemies, who must be beaten, be they evil thoughts and habits in himself, or spiritual wickednesses in high places, or Russians, or Border-ruffians, or Bill, Tom, or Harry, who will not let him live his life in quiet till he has thrashed them" (*School Days*, II, 5; 243).[10]

As to physical combat, far from advocating it for its own sake, Hughes takes pains to point out that it should normally be avoided, but that there are situations in which there is no acceptable alternative. When the Slogger lays violent hands on the smaller and weaker Arthur, Tom must rescue him, even if this means a fight, or else stand by and watch Arthur absorb a beating that he has done nothing to deserve. Those who accuse Hughes of arguing in favor of blind pugnaciousness need to look again at the final paragraph of the chapter:

As to fighting, keep out of it if you can, by all means. When the time comes, if it ever should, that you have to say 'Yes' or 'No' to a challenge to fight, say 'No' if you can—only take care you make it clear to yourselves why you say 'No.' It's a proof of the highest courage, if done from true Christian motives. It's quite right and justifiable, if done from a simple aversion to physical pain and danger. But don't say 'No' because you fear a licking, and say or think it's because you fear God, for that's neither Christian nor honest. And if you do fight, fight it out; and don't give in while you can stand and see. (*School Days*, II, 5; 260)

Even more rewarding as physical exercise than pugilism are the team sports played at Rugby. Speaking at the match that takes place on Tom's last day at school, the young master praises cricket for " 'the discipline and reliance on one another which it teaches.' " " 'It merges the individual in the eleven,' " he continues; " 'he doesn't play that he may win, but that his side may.' " Tom agrees, adding that " 'football and cricket ... are such much better games than fives or hare-and-hounds, or any others where the object is to come in first or to win for one's self' " (*School Days*, II, 8; 300). The lesson implicit in the triumph of Tom's side in the School-house football match on his first day at Rugby and articulated by Old Brooke at the singing that evening is here restated by Tom, who has by now succeeded to Brooke's wisdom as well as his position.

Teamwork, of course, involves much more than winning at cricket or football. The kind of cooperation called for on the playing field is also required if the school is to function successfully as a community. Everyone at Rugby—from the Doctor down through the masters and the prepostors to the lowliest and most ignorant fag—has a role to perform, and all must abide by the rules, which, as Arnold told Tom and East years ago, were set up for the general good and not in order to give one individual or group an unfair advantage over any other.

The American novelist and critic William Dean Howells was only partly correct in seeing in *Tom Brown's School Days* "the democratic spirit of the English schools, with their sense of equality and their honor of personal worth."[11] If Rugby is democratic and egalitarian, it is only in the sense that, theoretically at least, distinctions based on social class are obliterated or obscured and, as Howells says, "Tom Brown is the free and equal comrade of decent boys of whatever station"[12]—which, as we have seen, he has always been. In another sense, in its emphasis on hierarchy, the world of the nineteenth-century public school is something entirely different.

Now, a hierarchical system is not tyranny, in Hughes's view, if it is based on the genuine merit and achievements of those at the top and if they act in accordance with laws that are understood and accepted. Carlyle in his *Past and Present* called such worthy leaders "Real-Superiors." When all is well at Rugby, when the sixth-formers to whom Dr. Arnold delegates so much responsibility measure up to their obligations and enforce the rules, justice prevails. However, during periods when those whom Carlyle termed "Mock-Superiors" assume positions of authority, as happened in School-house following the departure of Brooke and his like-minded associates, chaos reigns and no boy is safe from cruelty and exploitation.

On the day of Tom's last cricket match, the young master draws an important parallel between the leadership of the team and the leadership of the school. Speaking of the captain of the cricket eleven, he says, " 'What a post is his in our School-world! almost as hard as the Doctor's; requiring skill and gentleness and firmness, and I know not what other rare qualities.' " Changing his emphasis to the headmaster's position, the young master goes on to an equally important analogy, between the governance of Rugby and the government of the nation. " 'What a sight it is . . . the Doctor as a ruler! Perhaps ours is the only little corner of the British Empire which is thoroughly, wisely, and strongly ruled just now' " (*School Days*, II, 8; 300).

In passages like this, it becomes apparent that Hughes is using *Tom Brown's School Days* to comment on political issues of the day. England is governed no better in 1857 than it was when the Christian Socialists began their movement nine years earlier. Able leadership is still urgently required, and people of all classes still need to come together in some kind of system that will foster fellow-feeling rather than antagonism. In a significant sense, the Rugby of this novel is far more than an Old Boy's nostalgic recollection of his public school as it was a generation ago: it is also his model of the well-governed society that must come into being in the future.

That society may or may not be socialist. Tom's disregard of class distinctions is certainly held up to the reader's admiration, but he shows none of the outright radicalism that is so prominent a feature of *Tom Brown at Oxford*. The prepostor Holmes seems to be swimming against the Rugby tide when he criticizes some younger boys for stealing poultry: " 'If the chickens were dead and lying in a shop, you wouldn't take them, I know that, any more than you would apples out of Griffith's basket; but there's no real difference between chickens running about and apples on a tree, and the same articles in a shop. I wish our morals were sounder in such matters. There's nothing so mischievous as these school distinctions, which jumble up right and wrong, and justify things in us for which poor boys would be sent to prison' " (*School Days*, II, 4; 240).

But if Rugby is indeed a model for the reorganization of society, clearly this will be along Christian lines. At no time did Arnold forget, or allow the masters and pupils at Rugby to forget, that religious principles were to be paramount at his school. That even Tom Brown comes under the Doctor's spell is a great tribute to the strength of Arnold's convictions and the eloquence of his preaching.

When East explains to Tom why he has not been confirmed, he says that he objects to the exclusiveness of Christianity as he understands it. " 'I don't want to be one of your saints, one of your elect, whatever the right phrase is. My sympathies are all the other way; with the many, the poor devils who run about the streets and don't go to church.' " Tom protests that " 'being confirmed and taking the Sacrament . . . makes you feel on the side of all the good and all the bad too, of everybody in the world. Only there's some great dark strong power, which is crushing you and everybody else. That's what Christ conquered and we've got to fight' " (*School Days*, II, 7; 287). Though Tom falters in his attempt to explain all this to East, the Doctor gets through to the confused youngster with no difficulty. Like Hughes's Christian Socialism, the view taken by Arnold, often termed the Broad Church position, stresses the unifying aspect of the national religion: there is a place in the community, whether that be the school or the nation, for each believer, regardless of the class to which he belongs or the particular tenets to which he subscribes.

Finally, Arnold's school inculcates what might be called a sacramental view of the world. Nothing in life, however humble or base, is without spiritual significance—a lesson that is dinned into Tom from his first Rugby Chapel sermon to his last conversation with the young master. From the small boy puzzling over his vulgus or the London tailor laboring in his sweatshop to the visionary who seeks to reform education or society, everyone in the world of the school and the great world beyond is confronted with innumerable challenges and can turn these into opportunities only with the aid of Christian faith.

The Scouring of the White Horse

Superficially viewed, Hughes's second novel appears to be a very different book from the Tom Brown stories that precede and follow it. The protagonist of *The Scouring of the White Horse* does not resemble the author; most of the action takes place in an isolated district of rural England rather than at a preeminent educational institution at the core of national life; and there is even less of a sustained and unified narrative than we find in Hughes's other two long works of fiction.

The Scouring of the White Horse is something of a hodgepodge— part love story, part reportage, part antiquarian lore, and part local color; and yet, despite its seeming lack of direction, it exudes an undeniable charm. Originally published late in 1858 for the Christmas trade, it so appealed to readers that a second edition was called for within a few weeks.[13] Most of the first reviewers were highly complimentary, two of them going so far as to compare Hughes's work favorably with Thackeray's.[14] Though *The Scouring of the White Horse* is virtually unknown today, it continues to have its admirers: for example one modern writer, who draws on it freely in compiling his guide to Berkshire, praises it warmly and says that "it is a book I keep by my bedside, to browse through in those delightful moments before sleep."[15]

After an initial chapter set in London, the novel takes us back to the Vale of the White Horse, where *Tom Brown's School Days* began; only now we see it not through the eyes of a native son but rather from the perspective of a confirmed city dweller, a twenty-one-year-old clerk. Young Richard is practical-minded, ambitious, and materialistic, earning extra money by his skill in shorthand, which he has learned in those spare hours that, as he sees it, his fellow clerks have frittered away in "reading poetry and other rubbish."[16]

Just as Richard is trying to decide where to go on his imminent annual holiday, he receives an invitation from a friend he made when both of them attended a commercial academy in the London suburb of Brentford. Now a farmer, Joe Hurst asks Richard to visit him during the festival that is about to take place in his part of Berkshire, and the thrifty Richard accepts, largely because spending two weeks with Joe at Elm Close Farm would cost him less money than any of the other trips he has been thinking about taking.

Richard initially has no great desire to attend the scouring of the White Horse. What can this traditional rustic celebration possibly mean to a hard-headed Londoner like himself? "I think Joe, and parties in the counties generally, set too much store by such things, and hold their noses much higher than they've any need to do, because their families have never cared to move about, and push on in the world, and so they know where their great-grandfathers were born" (*Scouring*, 18).

Richard sounds smug, but he actually possesses considerable intellectual curiosity. His first sight of the enormous monument intrigues him, and "the more I thought of this strange old White Horse, the more it took hold of me, and I resolved, if I could, while I was down in the country to learn all about it" (*Scouring*, 18). He will get whatever information he can from knowledgeable locals, and he will "be able to carry it all away" with no difficulty: his memory is excellent, he thinks with considerable self-satisfaction; and, besides, his skill in shorthand is such that he "can take down everything that is said as fast as most people can speak it" (*Scouring*, 18).

Having failed to extract anything of interest from the stolid Joe Hurst, Richard encounters an elderly gentleman on White Horse Hill who turns out to be a storehouse of local history and legend, and who is delighted to respond to Richard's many questions because, as he says, " 'it is seldom that I can get any of the youth of this day to take an interest in these matters, the study of which would greatly benefit their manners and morals' " (*Scouring*, 35).

This antiquary shares the belief commonly held in the Vale that the White Horse was carved out of the hillside by King Alfred, though he concedes that there may be merit in the argument of those who hold that it is actually hundreds of years older. The important thing is to remember and commemorate what Alfred and his brother Ethelred achieved by their triumph against the invaders: with the help of brave Berkshire men, they made a "gallant stand" at Ashdown that "probably saved England a hundred years of Paganism" (*Scouring*, 51).

Richard's informant is far more than a repository of dry historical facts. On the contrary, his attitude toward the past is suffused with deep emotion, and it is plain that he takes a very dim view of modern skepticism. The attitude of his contemporaries toward history and those who write it—their misguided preference for " 'the Edda, and all sorts of heathen stuff' " to the " 'godly books' " set down " 'by God-fearing men, who were not ashamed of the faith which was in them,' " " 'men who believed, Sir, that a living God was ruling in England, and that in His name one of them might defy a thousand' " (*Scouring*, 52)—he finds deplorable.

In an age when spiritual values are waning, it is difficult for historians or their readers to make what the antiquary considers to be appropriate judgments about the great men of the past. Nineteenth-century men and women can no longer see the significance in the story of Edmund, king of East Anglia, who suffered martyrdom in standing up to the Danes, unlike his brother Edwold, who beat a cowardly retreat to a monastery while the pagans despoiled his land and butchered his people;[17] they have forgotten " 'how terrible is Christ the Son of God in the counsels of men, and with what glorious triumph He adorns those whom He tries here under the name of suffering' " (*Scouring*, 42).

The worldly Richard, who has never before heard such talk, is deeply impressed. He acquires a different, but equally enlightening, perspective on the White Horse and its periodic scourings from another source, the Reverend Mr. Warton, now a London clergyman but formerly the local curate, who has returned to the Vale to attend the ceremony. With the parson's help, Richard pieces together information about most of the scourings held during the second half of the eighteenth century and the first half of the nineteenth, and in the process he arrives at some significant understanding about features of the festival that have endured as well as those that have changed.

In many ways, the scouring that Richard visits in 1857 remains a celebration of the people, a magnet drawing members of all the social classes. Lord Craven, the great aristocrat of the neighborhood, and his party are cheered on their arrival; the local squire is everywhere, making himself useful, not least as a peacemaker. Of course, most of the twenty thousand men, women, and children who mill around the eight acres of Uffington Castle to watch the games and shows, eat, drink, buy trinkets, and socialize are of considerably humbler standing. The sporting contests held in conjunction with the scouring are traditional: backswording, wrestling, jingling, and several kinds of racing—all minutely and lovingly described.

And yet something has changed, and not for the better. Richard comes across a handbill advertising the 1776 scouring, and the contrast between it and the one held in 1857 is instructive. The earlier event was much more casually put together, and the prizes advertised were farm implements, food, and clothing rather than cash. In other ways, too, commercialism has crept into the modern scouring. The parson points out to Richard that " 'the horse race for a silver cup has disappeared,' " and adds, with some irony: " 'Epsom and Ascot have swallowed up the little country races, just as big manufacturers swallow up little ones, and big shops whole streets of little shops, and nothing but monsters flourish in this age of unlimited competition and general enlightenment' " (*Scouring*, 91).

In chapters 6 and 7, Richard gives a detailed account of what he sees and hears on his first day at the "pastime." His second day on White Horse Hill is equally pleasant, but he says little about it: it is much like the first, he points out, and, moreover, "the gentlemen who are going to publish my story seem to think already that I am rather too long-winded" (*Scouring*, 177).

By the time we get to the eighth chapter, it is clear that a few days in Berkshire have effected a marked change in Richard. This "cockney," as Joe calls him (*Scouring*, 78), came to the country full of prejudices, but after his immersion in the ways of the Vale, as these have been displayed before him at the scouring of the White Horse, Richard finds himself taking an entirely different view of the world.

I had been bred up from a child never to look beyond my own narrow sphere. To get on in it was the purpose of my life, and I had drilled myself into despising everything which did not, as I thought, help towards this end. . . . I must have been getting to be a very narrow, bigoted, disagreeable sort of fellow, and it was high time that I should find my way to Elm Close, or some such place, to have my eyes opened a little, and discover that a man may work just as steadily and honestly—aye, much more steadily and honestly—at his own business, without shutting up his brains and his heart against everything else that is going on in the world around him. (*Scouring*, 177–78)

Richard's "eyes," "his brains and his heart," have indeed been opened. He has, as we have noticed, gained a genuine appreciation of the values inherent in rural traditions. He has also overcome the bias prevalent in his radical London debating society against the aristocracy and landed gentry: having seen the enthusiastic reception accorded Lord Craven at the scouring, and having watched the energetic and resourceful squire in action before and during the festival, he no longer believes that members of those classes are cruel, idle, and debauched enemies of the poor.

The kind of growth Richard has undergone is clearly intended by Hughes to teach his readers a lesson. As he says in the preface to *The Scouring of the White Horse*, "We are sure that reverence for all great Englishmen, and a loving remembrance of the great deeds done by them in old times, will help to bring to life in us the feeling that we are a family, bound together to work out God's purposes in this little island, and in the uttermost parts of the earth; to make clear to us the noble inheritance which we have in common; and to sink into their proper place the miserable trifles, and odds and ends, over which we are so apt to wrangle" (*Scouring*, x). Especially in an era when the classes are growing apart and individuals in different walks of life are becoming estranged from one another, it is essential that those elements in the national heritage that unify rather than divide people be kept firmly in mind.

Something quite different also happens to Richard during his sojourn in the Vale: he falls in love. As soon as he sees Joe's sister Lucy, Richard is smitten; and—despite petty jealousies, minor misunderstandings, and the difference between his background and hers—there is every indication as the novel closes that his suit will prosper. Bent on self-improvement, Richard has had no time for romance during his working life in London, and it is no accident that his emotional awakening coincides with the broadening of his social and spiritual horizons.

Richard returns to London a new man, having "learnt to look beyond his own narrow cellar in the great world-city, to believe in other things than cash payments and short-hand for making his cellar liveable in, to have glimpses of and to sympathise with the life of other men, in his own time, and in the old times before him" (*Scouring*, 198). During the last stage of his journey back to the capital, having drunk a couple of glasses of ale while his train made a brief stop at Reading, he has a dream not unlike George Arthur's

vision in *Tom Brown's School Days*—a dream that teaches him to
appreciate the true significance of work, which is not mere money-
grubbing drudgery, as he believed, but rather the divinely ordained
means of conquering time and death, of leaving behind us, when our
time runs out and we do die, a legacy that may be less enduring than
the Berkshire White Horse or less inspiring than the fabled exploits
of Alfred or Edmund, but one that will nevertheless make a difference to those who survive us.

Like *Tom Brown's School Days*, then, *The Scouring of the White
Horse* celebrates the virtues of living one's life firmly rooted in history,
tradition, and a sense of place, with a full heart and an ardent spirit,
in a society that is an organic whole rather than a mechanical aggre-
gation of clashing values and interests. The social harmony that
Hughes advocates, here as elsewhere in his work, must rest on consensus—a voluntary consensus if at all possible, but if necessary a
consensus embodied in just laws justly enforced.

The last point is made most clearly in what *The Scouring of the
White Horse* has to say about the country sports of backswording and
wrestling. Lucy believes that it is wrong for men to engage in these
forms of combat. Richard, as part of his campaign to win her favor,
at first sides with her and against her brother Joe, who argues " 'that
they are old English games, and we sets great store by them down
here, though some of our folk as ought to know better does set their
faces against them now-a-days' " (*Scouring*, 79). His curiosity aroused
once again, Richard asks both Warton and a doctor whom he meets
at the scouring what they think of such contests, and, though the
answers he extracts from them are generally favorable to these amuse-
ments, the point is not clinched until the parson's sermon that concludes the novel.

Celebrations like the scouring of the White Horse, Warton says
there, are the Lord's: God intended them to be "feasts for the whole
nation—for the rich and the poor, the free man and the slave" (*Scouring*, 203), and they must be religious as well as secular occasions. The
rougher games that have lately been criticized by many, including
some clergymen, he continues in language reminiscent of *Tom Brown's
School Days*, play an important role in such divinely sanctioned festivals: "The object of wrestling and of all other athletic sports is to
strengthen men's bodies, and to teach them to use their strength
readily, to keep their tempers, to endure fatigue and pain. These are

all noble ends, my brethren. God gives us few more valuable gifts than strength of body, and courage, and endurance—to you labouring men they are beyond all price. We ought to cultivate them in all right ways, for they are given us to protect the weak, to subdue the earth, to fight for our homes and country if necessary" (*Scouring*, 210).

But these sports need to be more strictly regulated, the parson insists. Under the watchful eye of resolute umpires, the participants must subordinate their animal instincts to rules that guarantee fair play. To suppress such drives, which are necessary and healthy, would make them less than men; to give these impulses free rein, by resorting to excessive violence or outright brutality, would lead to anarchy. In this sense, the stage where backswording and wrestling contests are held is not really very different from the playing fields of Rugby or, for that matter, from the arena in which the social and political life of the nation runs its course.

Tom Brown at Oxford

Both Alexander Macmillan, Hughes's publisher, and Hughes himself regarded *Tom Brown at Oxford* as a "continuation" of *Tom Brown's School Days*,[18] but from the beginning readers were struck by the differences between Hughes's third novel and his first. As the reviewer in *Blackwood's Edinburgh Magazine*—writing in February 1861, while *Tom Brown at Oxford* was still being serialized in *Macmillan's Magazine*—pointed out, in *Tom Brown's School Days* Hughes had been a pioneer, "the Columbus of the world of schoolboy romance," whereas in this sequel he was "no longer breaking new ground. Sketches of college life had been done before, with more or less success, and nothing very new could be said about it; nor does it seem to offer any great facilities for a continuous story."[19]

Indeed, *Tom Brown at Oxford* is not a "continuous story," not even in the rudimentary sense that another early reviewer had in mind when he said that "it simply records the life an Oxford youth during the three years of his undergraduateship."[20] Of its fifty chapters, approximately half deal with Tom's freshman year; a single chapter (35) treats his second year and another (42) his third; during chapter 44, he returns to Oxford for three weeks in order to meet the residence requirement for the M.A. degree; and the rest of the novel, including several chapters from which Tom is absent, is set in Berkshire or London during summer vacations or after he has left the university.

The irregular and rather rickety structure of *Tom Brown at Oxford* is only one reason why it falls short of the effect, and the effectiveness, of *Tom Brown's School Days*, itself far from a totally coherent piece of fiction. In Hughes's first novel, his protagonist matures under the guidance of the self-assured Dr. Arnold and the stable George Arthur in the tonic atmosphere of Rugby School. In *Tom Brown at Oxford*, by contrast, Tom's chief mentor has serious problems of his own and does not make Tom over according to his own example, even though Tom does admire him greatly. As to Oxford, Tom's view of that institution is considerably more ambivalent than his attitude toward Rugby in the earlier work. Also, during and immediately after his university years he is frequently afflicted with a sense of guilt that is more debilitating than any such feeling he harbored at school. Tom suffers much, learns much, but also unlearns much; and the reader, who has watched him try out and reject one approach to life after another, closes the book with little sense of having witnessed the sort of instructive character development to be found in *Tom Brown's School Days*. Indeed, it is not unfair to say that we leave Tom Brown at the end of the Oxford novel as dissatisfied and confused as we found him at the beginning.

Seven months after leaving Rugby, Tom enters St. Ambrose's, an Oxford college considered to be "as distinguished for learning, morality, and respectability, as any in the University" (*Oxford*, 3). On all three counts, however, the quality of the student body has recently undergone a steep decline. A substantial portion of the undergraduates now consists of "gentlemen-commoners," the sons of rich aristocrats and squires, who pay double fees and in return are entitled to various special privileges and immunities. Along with their less wealthy followers, the gentlemen-commoners form the "fast set" that dominates the social life of St. Ambrose's and displays a marked aversion to studying.

Tom falls in with this set soon after his arrival when he attends a breakfast party in the lavish rooms of one Drysdale, "the heir of an old as well as of a rich family" (*Oxford*, 22), whom he met at a country house a few weeks earlier. Huge quantities of expensive food, drink, and tobacco are consumed at this gathering, and Tom is appalled by the mixture of superciliousness and vulgarity displayed by the guests.

But anti-intellectualism and gluttony are only two of the failings of the fast set. Its members spend much of their time gambling and, as Tom learns later, wenching; they run up extravagant bills with Oxford and London tradesmen; and, as a consequence of their financial and other excesses, they frequently fall into the clutches of usurious moneylenders. They hold the college rules in contempt; and, even though the St. Ambrose's authorities are inclined to treat them gently, they are often in disciplinary trouble.

As a result of his interest and skill in sports, Tom soon comes to the attention of another prominent group, the "boating set," whose great object is to uphold the honor of St. Ambrose's in the college races that are held on the river each spring. Though Tom is an inexperienced oarsman, he gets a place on the St. Ambrose's crew, which does extremely well during his initial year as a member, thanks to long hours of practice and a merciless training regimen.

Rowing in the "eight" affords Tom welcome physical exercise, subjects him to the kind of discipline in which he came to believe at school through his involvement in football and cricket, and gives him a share in the triumph of victory. But his first year at Oxford does not yield Tom many other satisfactions.

Though he gets on well enough with the fast set, its carousing, unruliness, and snobbery do not really appeal to him. Tom misses the responsibility that his status as a prepostor conferred on him at Rugby; and, because the freshman curriculum at Oxford presents him with no great challenge, he finds his studies, such as they are, boring. As he complains to Arthur in the first letter he writes from St. Ambrose's, " 'it's an awfully idle place' " (*Oxford*, 6).

The best thing that happens to Tom during that first year is his making friends with Hardy, a servitor: that is, a poor but deserving student who pays no fees, working his way through college by doing a variety of menial jobs. Proud, shy, and touchy, Hardy is virtually ostracized by most of the well-to-do and class-conscious St. Ambrose's men, but Tom does not share their bias. "He had not been instructed at home to worship mere conventional distinctions of rank or wealth, and had gone to a school which was not frequented by persons of rank, and where no one knew whether a boy was heir to a principality, or would have to fight his own way in the world" (*Oxford*, 40).

They meet when the cocky Tom, sure of his ability to handle a boat, comes to grief the first time he takes out a skiff by himself and Hardy rescues him, giving the now chastened freshman some rowing pointers on the way back from this embarrassing expedition. Superb oarsman though Hardy is, however, most of the lessons he teaches Tom, that first year and later, have nothing to do with boating. Like Tom, Hardy is dissatisfied with much at Oxford and St. Ambrose's, but he has thought through his objections more carefully and is able to give the younger man some insight into the reasons for the intellectual and moral sterility that prevails there.

According to Hardy, who has obviously read and been influenced by Carlyle, the trouble with the university is basically spiritual. Though lip-service is given to Christianity, the religion that is preached at Oxford tends to be arid and lifeless, devoid of any real connection with the practice of the institution or its members. Almost everyone seems to have forgotten the lofty goals the university was created to meet. It is no longer a community of scholars in search of truth that will help mankind and glorify God; rather, it has deteriorated into " 'a sort of learning machine, in which I am to grind for three years to get certain degrees which I want' " (*Oxford*, 70).

During a discussion of the Punic Wars, Hardy shows Tom how meaningful and how applicable to contemporary problems apparently arcane learning can be. If approached thoughtfully and even reverently, the study of ancient history need not be dry and dull, Hardy maintains: unlike their Roman adversaries, " 'the Carthaginians were nothing but a great trading aristocracy . . . a dirty, bargain-driving, buy-cheap-and-sell-dear aristocracy—of whom the world was well rid,' " and nineteenth-century Englishmen, pondering the meaning of Carthage's decline, must ask themselves how their increasingly commercial nation can escape a similar disaster. " 'I think that successful trade is our rock ahead. The devil who holds new markets and twenty per cent. profits in his gift is the devil that England has most to fear from.' " Only true religion can save the country from this menacing devil, " 'but this work of making trade righteous, of Christianizing trade, looks like the very hardest the Gospel has ever had to take in hand—in England at any rate' " (*Oxford*, 100–101).

Naturally, Hardy is outraged by the behavior of the fast set, whose members care nothing for either the spirit or the intellect, regarding the university as nothing more than a glorified playground. When Tom seems on the verge of emulating these contemptible creatures— too old to act like boys, too irresponsible to conduct themselves like men—by carrying on an affair with a barmaid at a pub frequented by the St. Ambrose's crew, it is Hardy, with some unexpected help from the gentleman-commoner Drysdale, who dissuades him, pointing out that by cultivating a relationship that can have no acceptable outcome, marriage with such a girl being out of the question, Tom is playing " 'the devil's game' " (*Oxford*, 169).

Thus, in addition to clarifying Tom's intellectual position and strengthening the democratic strain in the Toryism Tom has inherited from his father, Hardy pulls him through the great moral crisis of his first year. He is also responsible for a change in Tom's rather rigid religious attitudes.

While Tom is an undergraduate, the university is still trying to come to terms with the High-Church teachings of the so-called Oxford or Tractarian Movement of the 1830s and 1840s, led by John Henry Newman, John Keble, and Edward Bouverie Pusey. After Tom gets his first extensive exposure to their ideas at a wine party he attends, he tells Hardy how repellent he finds Tractarianism: " 'it seems to me all a Gothic-mouldings and man-millinery business' " (*Oxford*, 87).

Certainly no Tractarian himself, Hardy hears Tom out in amused silence, only interjecting an ironic comment now and then. Before he has a chance to give Tom his own view of the Oxford Movement, they are joined by a member of the "High-Church set," a studious young man named Grey who has been reading history with Hardy. Tom's prejudice against Grey and his friends is softened when he learns that Grey has started teaching in a night school for poor town boys set up by a local curate, and—his better nature and his desire to be of service to those less fortunate than himself having been aroused—he instantly offers to aid Grey in this work, a proposal that the startled Grey declines. As soon as Grey leaves, Hardy breaks out in laughter: " 'that don't look as if it were all mere Gothic-mouldings and man-millinery, does it?' " (*Oxford*, 89), he says to a subdued Tom. More seriously, Hardy points out that Grey and his High-Church friends, misguided though they may be, do serve an important function at St. Ambrose's because of their " 'protest for self-denial, and against self-indulgence, which is nowhere more needed than here' " (*Oxford*, 90).

Though Tom never becomes seriously interested in the Oxford Movement, his withdrawal from the affair with Patty the barmaid does show that he has taken to heart Hardy's words about self-denial and self-indulgence, and he soon manages to persuade Grey to let him help with his religiously motivated teaching mission. The work is difficult and unpleasant, but it gives Tom a kind of satisfaction that he has never experienced before while at the university.

As Tom's freshman year draws to a close, he is delighted by Hardy's strong performance in the final examination for his degree and dismayed by the debauchery and vandalism of which most of the other college men are guilty following a series of riotous end-of-term parties. St. Ambrose's has sunk into the kind of anarchy that comes about when the effective exercise of authority has broken down. "Even in St. Ambrose's, reckless and vicious as the college had become, by far the greater part of the undergraduates would gladly have seen a change in the direction of order and decency, and were sick of the wretched licence of doing right in their own eyes, and wrong in every other person's" (*Oxford*, 264).

The year ends on a happier note, with the pomp and gaiety of the Commemoration ceremonies and a flurry of related social events. Among the many visitors who crowd into Oxford for this annual celebration is Tom's uncle, Robert Winter, a valetudinarian clergyman from Berkshire, accompanied by his daughter Katie and Katie's cousin on her mother's side, the sprightly Mary Porter, whom Tom has not known before. Tom and Mary are immediately attracted to each other, and they arrange to meet again during the long vacation that is about to begin.

That summer, however, turns out to be something quite different from the idyllic succession of country-house visits to which Tom has been looking forward. He does go to stay at Barton Manor, the place in Berkshire that Mary's father has rented, where he "is acknowledged as a cousin by Mr. and Mrs. Porter" (*Oxford*, 328), and his parents reciprocate by inviting the Porters, including Mary, to visit them. Tom also makes two trips to Englebourn, the village where his uncle is nominally the rector even though all the work of the parish is done by a curate while Mr. Winter frets about his health, and it is there that things begin to go seriously wrong for Tom.

At Englebourn, Tom finds himself drawn into the unhappy situation of the Winburn family, formerly residents of Tom's native village. There are only two Winburns left now: a poor sick widow who is nursed by Katie Winter and the old woman's son Harry, with whom Tom had played when both were boys. After Dame Winburn dies, Harry is evicted from their cottage, and Tom's efforts to help his old friend are unavailing. The rector's prickly gardener, Simon, turns a deaf ear to Tom's proposal that he take Harry on as his assistant, and the brutish Squire Wurley rejects Tom's offer to rent the Winburns' cottage for Harry.

Already chastened by these failures, Tom is horrified by the disclosure that Patty, the barmaid with whom he carried on a flirtation at Oxford, is Simon's daughter and Harry's sweetheart. Though that affair is over, Tom believes with good reason that he has inadvertently injured Harry and also damaged his own reputation in the eyes of the Porters, Mary's parents and Mary herself, who realize that there must have been something between Tom and the girl but draw the wrong conclusion about the nature of that actually quite innocent relationship.

Back at Oxford for his second year, Tom is deeply unsettled by the unpromising state of his suit of Mary Porter and by the damage that his self-esteem has suffered during the long vacation. He is also even more dissatisfied with his society than he had been as a freshman, only now he questions not so much the manners and morals of his fellow-undergraduates as the nature of a class system in which an able-bodied young man like Harry Winburn can get neither work nor justice. Invoking a famous phrase of Carlyle's, Tom generalizes Harry's plight into "the condition-of-England problem," and his perplexity over this becomes "every day more and more urgent and importunate, shaking many old beliefs, and leading him whither he knew not" (*Oxford*, 393).

On the advice of his college tutor, Tom first looks for a solution in the writings of the currently fashionable economists, adherents of Jeremy Bentham's Utilitarian views and believers in the necessity of limiting population as advocated by the Reverend Thomas Malthus. Though he initially finds their teachings plausible, Tom soon rejects them: "when he came to take stock of his newly-acquired knowledge, to weigh it and measure it, and found it to consist of a sort of hazy conviction that society would be all right and ready for the millennium, when every man could do what he liked, and nobody could interfere with him, and there should be a law against marriage, the result was more than he could stand" (*Oxford*, 393–94).

Nor are the High-Church doctrines of Grey and his set very helpful to Tom in his present predicament. Tom admires their faith and the dedication with which they strive to put their principles into practice, but he recoils from their notion that there is a gulf between the world in which men live and work, which they regard as the devil's, and the world of the spirit, which is God's. Held back by reservations reminiscent of East's in *Tom Brown's School Days*, Tom is unable to accept a church that views itself as "an exclusive body, which took no care of any but its own people" (*Oxford*, 395).

Tom's confusion seems to end when Hardy gives him a new book he has just finished reading, *Past and Present.* Carlyle, Tom discovers with awe and delight, speaks directly to his disenchantment with laissez-faire economics and points out that, even though it is necessary to take a spiritual view of the world, a withdrawal into sectarian isolation is dangerous and self-defeating. "The help which he had found was just what he wanted. There was no narrowing of the ground here—no appeal to men as members of any exclusive body whatever to separate themselves and come out of the devil's world; but to men as men, to every man as a man—to the weakest and meanest, as well as the strongest and most noble—telling them that the world is God's world, that every one of them has a work in it, and bidding them find their work and set about it" (*Oxford*, 396).

But Tom's temperament is still too mercurial to allow him to find anything like lasting peace of mind even in the teachings of a sage as eloquent and persuasive as Carlyle. His continuing involvement with Harry Winburn leads him, by the time he is in his third year at Oxford, to thoughts and deeds that are far more extreme than any advocated by the author of *Past and Present.*

During the summer after his second year, Tom catches Harry poaching. The Victorian establishment takes a very serious view of this offense, but, as Tom realizes, men like Harry are driven to it not by innate viciousness or an abstract contempt for the sanctity of private property but rather by simple hunger, brought on by their inability to find a lawful way to earn a living. The imprudent and naively idealistic Tom, whose "castle-building power" (*Oxford*, 431) is formidable, thinks that if he persuades Harry to give up poaching and sees to it that the village of Englebourn is made to understand why Harry has been indulging in this crime, the slate will be wiped clean and Tom's uncle, the rector, will help Harry get a fresh start. Tom is wrong, however: the squire has Harry arrested, and, after a trial, the unfortunate young man is sentenced to three months in jail. The result of this episode and Tom's consequent disillusionment is that he turns into "little better than a physical force Chartist at the age of twenty-one" (*Oxford*, 437).

Indeed, on his return to Oxford for his third and last undergraduate year, Tom is known as "Chartist" Brown. He now belongs to a radical set whose members indulge in a "cloud of sophisms, and plati-

tudes, and big one-sided ideas half-mastered," but Tom at least is motivated by principles that have been bred into him from his earliest
days: "a true and broad sympathy for men as men, and especially for
poor men as poor men, and a righteous and burning hatred against all
laws, customs, or notions, which, according to his light, either were
or seemed to be setting aside, or putting anything else in the place
of, or above the man" (*Oxford*, 459).

These views soon lead Tom to extralegal action. That October, he
goes to Harry Winburn's rescue when, once again, his friend is in
trouble with the authorities. After his release from prison, Harry takes
part in a riot during which some unemployed agricultural workers
smash machinery belonging to an old adversary of Harry's, and Tom
helps him escape from his pursuers.

It soon becomes clear, however, that Chartist radicalism is no more
satisfactory for Tom than any other philosophy he has tried and
found wanting. For one thing, Tom's family and his closest friends
disapprove of his new ideas, and Tom is not prepared to cut himself
off from them for the sake of those beliefs.

Squire Brown, for instance, is appalled when he visits Tom at Oxford and sees how his son has changed the decor of his rooms in
order to make a truculent political statement: a portrait of John
Milton—a follower of the seventeenth-century Puritan revolution and
an apologist for regicide—has replaced an engraving of George III
over Tom's mantelpiece, and this is flanked by reproductions of the
Magna Charta and, most offensive of all, the death warrant of King
Charles I.

In deference to his father, Tom throws the death warrant into the
fire, insisting, however, that though he " 'was deeply grieved at having given him pain, he could not and would not give up his honest
convictions, or pretend that they were changed, or even shaken' "
(*Oxford*, 465). For his part, Squire Brown does come to realize "that
the world has changed a good deal since his time" (*Oxford*, 466),
and that it is possible, and perhaps even necessary, for young men of
good will in the 1840s to espouse causes that were totally unacceptable in the England of his own youth, when respectable public
opinion was still stunned by the excesses of the French Revolution.

Tom's Rugby friend East—home on leave from India, where he
has been serving as an army officer—is Tom's unwilling accomplice
in his successful attempt to keep Harry Winburn out of the clutches
of the law, and, as he had done at school, East provides some down-to-

earth commentary on Tom's idealistic excesses. " 'He always was a headstrong beggar,' " East muses at one point. " 'What was it he was holding forth about last night? Let's see. "The sacred right of insurrection." Yes, that was it, and he talked as if he believed it all too; and, if there should be a row, which don't seem unlikely, by Jove I think he'd act on it in the sort of temper he's in. How about the sacred right of getting hung or transported? I shouldn't wonder to hear of that some day' " (*Oxford*, 439).

As always, too, Hardy, now a tutor at St. Ambrose's, serves as a restraining influence on Tom. Hardy shows his impetuous young friend that there is a fundamental inconsistency between the universal democracy advocated by the Chartists and Carlyle's doctrine of hero worship, and that history is full of examples contradicting the seductive notion that "the *vox populi* is the best test for finding your best man" (*Oxford*, 462).

Finally, Tom's romantic interest in Mary Porter helps to temper his political extremism. Katie Winter, who has been acting as Tom's advocate with Mary, is clearly displeased by his writing for a radical publication, the *Wessex Freeman*. At her request, he stops sending her copies, and ultimately he ceases contributing to it, though he insists to Hardy that " 'I'm not ashamed of what I wrote in that paper' " (*Oxford*, 502).

Tom's courtship of Mary has not prospered. The senior Porters' objections to the match, initially based on the youth of the couple, have been reinforced first by their discovery that Tom has been involved with Patty and more recently by the lies that Piers St. Cloud, a gentleman-commoner at St. Ambrose's with designs of his own on Mary, has been telling them about Tom's loose principles and wild behavior. But everything is straightened out when another member of Tom's college, Drysdale, defends Tom to Mr. Porter against St. Cloud's slanders, and when Mary and her father happen to see Tom at work with the children in a school for the poor that Grey has been running in London. On the verge of emigrating to New Zealand, Tom receives an invitation to call at the Porters' house, and it is soon made clear that all obstacles to a union between Tom and Mary have been removed.

Tom Brown at Oxford concludes with the protagonist a married man—a poor man, and also one who is still quite unsure as to what to do about the wrongs of his society and his own shortcomings. Only two things are certain: that, whatever course of action Tom decides to follow, he will have the support of Mary, who insists that, as a woman and his wife, she is fully capable of meeting all challenges by his side; and that, come what may, they will lead their lives in the world together "as the children of the Maker and Lord of it, their Father" (*Oxford*, 546).

Like *Tom Brown's School Days* and *The Scouring of the White Horse, Tom Brown at Oxford* is fundamentally a spiritual, intellectual, and moral biography of its protagonist during a crucial phase of his life. But, except for Tom's rededication to an all-embracing if vaguely defined Christianity, he has achieved no comprehensive world view by the time the novel ends.

Though this lack of resolution may be regarded as an aesthetic defect, it is not really a fatal flaw. On the completion of his university education in the mid-1840s, Tom Brown stands at the threshold of an uncertain, possibly even a dangerous, adult life. Hughes's first readers in *Macmillan's Magazine* in 1859–61 were surely well aware that a young Englishman of Tom's generation would have had to face many trials during the decade and a half after his departure from Oxford and that his ideas and attitudes would inevitably have undergone further changes in response to these challenges.

Neither the victory of free trade with the repeal of the Corn Laws in 1846 nor the last spasm of Chartism two years later led to the social harmony for which Tom had yearned. If the 1850s were ushered in with the euphoria surrounding the Great Exhibition at the Crystal Palace, they were soon disfigured by the national agony of the Crimean War. There had appeared no religious answer to the condition-of-England question, even Christian Socialism having proved to be inadequate; and, by the time *Tom Brown at Oxford* was completed, Anglican orthodoxy, which had been under attack for decades, was even more gravely threatened by the ideas contained in such controversial new books as *The Origin of Species* and *Essays and Reviews*, which will be discussed in the next chapter.

To leave Tom still uncertain and in search of specific answers at the conclusion of the novel, then, was a realistic gesture, even an act of courage, rather than a sign of artistic weakness on Hughes's part. And there are at least two general principles to which Tom Brown, very much like Tom Hughes himself, does clearly subscribe at this stage of his life.

The first is the conviction that there is a spiritual basis to existence, in each individual and in each community, such as a university or an entire nation. Materialism, which ignores this vital truth, leads to all kinds of evil consequences, whether in the form of "the flunkeyism and money-worship" of which Hardy complains during Tom's "master's term" at Oxford (*Oxford*, 500) or in the form of class conflict, which may not always arise from unworthy motives but which does invariably nurture bitterness and divisiveness.

The second is the conviction that, however damaging modern assaults on traditional religion may be, Christianity still has an essential role to play, only this must be a Christianity of the people rather than a Christianity of the cloister. Those who attempt to apply Christian principles to everyday life may have to endure the strictures of the orthodox and the jeers of the unbelieving, but they must not let such objections deter from their task.

In the preface to the sixth edition of *Tom Brown's School Days*, Hughes took note of the complaint that there was " 'too much preaching' " in his first novel. This charge gave him no concern: "Why, my whole object in writing at all," he asserted, "was to get the chance of preaching!"[21] However, even though not only *Tom Brown's School Days* but also its two successors are strongly didactic, as we have seen, there is a good deal more to them than "preaching." Hughes often displays genuine skill in setting his scenes, rendering his conversations, and moving his action along; and, even though his novels are indifferently constructed as wholes,[22] individual episodes—and, in the case of *Tom Brown at Oxford*, the only one to be published serially, individual installments—hang together quite effectively.

Hughes may not have been a master novelist, a rank to which he never aspired, but nonetheless his three works of book-length fiction, if approached with an open mind, can still offer readers not only instruction about the state of England and some of the country's institutions at the middle of the nineteenth century but also considerable delight.

Chapter Three

Faith, Church, and Christ

Though Christian Socialism as an organized movement ceased to exist after 1854, Thomas Hughes continued to devote himself to social reform in general and to the well-being of the working class in particular until the end of his long life. A strong religious element always pervaded his efforts, but for Hughes Christianity was far more than a spiritual force to enlighten and energize the cooperative and trade-union movements with which he worked or to justify the social legislation that he sponsored. The Christian faith, the established Church of England, and Jesus Christ—as the son of God but also and especially as the supreme example and inspiration to humankind—were all vitally significant to Hughes in their own terms, particularly as the nature and the role of each came increasingly under scrutiny during the 1860s and 1870s.[1] Characteristically forthright, Hughes's public utterances about these subjects took the form not only of speeches and lectures but also of the three books to be discussed in this chapter: *Religio Laici* (1861), *The Old Church* (1878), and *The Manliness of Christ* (1879).

Religio Laici

Hughes's *Religio Laici* grew directly out of the furor that broke out in England following the publication of *Essays and Reviews* (1860), a volume in which seven eminent academics and clergymen attempted to show how Christianity might be reconciled with the discoveries of nineteenth-century science, church history, and biblical criticism. Though they worked independently of one another and took very different paths, these writers had one aim in common: "to enquire what must be done if Christianity were to survive among thoughtful people."[2] In retrospect, that may seem a constructive and laudable goal; but at the time—a period of bitter religious controversy and, therefore, of defensiveness and even doubt among the faithful—the beleaguered leadership of the Church of England took a very different view of the book and ideas it contained.

The orthodox assault on *Essays and Reviews* was led by Samuel Wilberforce, Bishop of Oxford. He persuaded his fellow-bishops to condemn the book in February 1861; somewhat later, 11,000 clergymen and 137,000 laymen signed an address declaring their hostility to what they regarded as its heretical message. Two contributors to *Essays and Reviews*, Rowland Williams and Henry Bristow Wilson, were actually put on trial for heresy by a church court, convicted, and stripped of their clerical offices for one year, but this verdict was subsequently overturned as the result of an appeal to the Judicial Committee of the Privy Council.

Though Thomas Arnold had been dead for nearly two decades when *Essays and Reviews* was published, his large shadow hung over both the book itself and the controversy to which it gave rise. The first essay in the volume, "The Education of the World," was the work of Frederick Temple, then serving as one of Arnold's successors as headmaster of Rugby. Arnold's disciple and biographer A. P. Stanley wrote the most eloquent defense of *Essays and Reviews* and the most thoughtful indictment of its critics, arguing that those who diverged from orthodoxy, narrowly defined, should not be censured and that freedom of inquiry was both healthy in itself and necessary. Stanley also pointed out that "all the fundamental principles of the present volume" had their counterparts in Arnold's work.[3] The third public figure associated with Arnold to enter the lists was Thomas Hughes.

Like Stanley, Hughes deplored any attempt to condemn, much less to silence, devout seekers after truth who sought to put Christianity and the Church of England on what they believed to be an intellectually sounder footing. On the other hand, he agreed with those critics of *Essays and Reviews* who held that the ideas it expressed, whatever the good intentions of the authors, might well be destructive of faith. What was needed at this difficult time was an affirmative credo appealing to, and articulating the position of, " 'men of all parties in the Church with any living faith in them and not fearfully clinging on to the letter and disregarding the spirit.' "[4] He soon found his opportunity to make such a statement.

F. D. Maurice had also been deeply troubled by *Essays and Reviews* and the debates that ensued on its publication, and he freely expressed his concerns to his friends.[5] Looking to Maurice for guidance throughout, some of those who had been associated with him in the Christian Socialist movement accordingly resolved in March 1861 to issue "a set of papers ... bearing on the religious questions treated of in 'Essays and Reviews,' but considered from a strictly positive point of view.... The writers ... will all be members of the Church of England, not mere attendants at her services, but men who, from very different starting-points, have been led to feel that her ritual is the truest embodiment of our national worship."[6]

The title chosen for the series, "Tracts for Priests and People," was Maurice's; the editors were Hughes and J. Llewelyn Davies. There were ultimately fifteen of these tracts, published at a shilling each by Macmillan; Hughes's *Religio Laici*, published in May 1861, was the first to appear.

Hughes makes it very clear at the outset of *Religio Laici* that his tract is a response not only to *Essays and Reviews* but also to the debate aroused by that volume and to the underlying causes of that debate. He believes that the aim of the authors of the *Essays and Reviews* has been misconstrued: it was not "to set up any deistic or pantheistic philosophy in the place of Christianity," but rather "to claim for English Churchmen the right of honest and free inquiry in the realm of nature and the history of man as a necessary step to the spread of a spiritual Christianity."[7] They have not, he concedes, gone about this task in the right way, and their approaches to it have left them open to misunderstanding, even though Hughes, for one, does not find in the collection what many readers claim to see there: a rejection of miracles, for instance, or of "the notion of a domain of intellect and knowledge, in which man can and may use his reason" separate from "a boundless region of spiritual things beyond, which is the sole dominion of faith"; a rejection of "Prophecy"; a rejection of the "Inspiration of Scripture"; a rejection of " 'creation' " in the face of the work of modern scientists (*Religio*, 12–13).

The possibility, even the likelihood, that some of their ideas may be infelicitously expressed or downright mistaken, however, should not give rise to alarm. What is alarming to Hughes is "the dishonesty of the attempts which have been made to put them down, and to stifle free inquiry" (*Religio*, 9). But this kind of overreaction by bishops and other clergy, if reprehensible and dangerous, is also very under-standable, for it is becoming increasingly clear that in the early 1860s the issue is no longer one of mere doctrinal differences among churchmen or Christians: by now, the question has come down to "the very foundations of faith and human life," so much so that it has become necessary to ask if indeed there is "a faith for mankind" (*Religio*, 8).

There is no doubt in Hughes's mind that religious skepticism is growing, especially among young men, the future leaders of society. It is essential, "for the sake of England" (*Religio*, 10), that this skepticism be addressed: not by those who obviously have a vested interest in the preservation of the church establishment, or by those whose arguments are marred by partisanship or pedantry, but rather by those who speak simply and honestly from simple and honest religious conviction. Hughes casts himself as that sort of spokesman, starting with his choice of title: "a layman's faith."[8]

Hughes begins by asking what would follow if the worst fears of those who have, according to him, misread *Essays and Reviews* were realized, and if the whole idea of revealed religion were abandoned in response to the positions supposedly taken in that volume. His short answer is that there would probably not be much change, and it would certainly not be change for the better.

If, for example, it were agreed that nature operates according to laws discoverable by science, a question would immediately arise: who established those laws? Hughes is ready with his answer: though he is as willing as any scientist to "acknowledge a permanent order, physical laws," he believes "them to be the expressions of a living and a righteous will; I believe a holy and true God to be behind them, therefore, I can sit down humbly, and try to understand them, and when I understand, to obey" (*Religio*, 15).

What kind of laws are these, and what kind of obedience do they exact? Not "dead laws," which "are, so far as I can see, just what I, and you, and all mankind, have been put into this world to fight against" (*Religio*, 16): not laws, in other words, that we are obliged to follow blindly, regardless of the consequences. Do we not eliminate weeds that flourish naturally, and do we not build houses that stand despite the law of gravity? Above all, does the fact that we acknowledge the "law of death" (*Religio*, 16) mean that we bow before it? Not at all. "I utterly hate it. No noble or true work is done in this world except in direct defiance of it. What is to become of the physician's work, of every effort at sanitary reform, of every attempt at civilizing and raising the poor and the degraded, if we are to sit down and submit ourselves to this law?" (*Religio*, 17).

But just as there are laws governing natural forces, so there are laws governing human behavior, one of which is that there is an apparently ineradicable superstitious dimension to the way our minds work. Men have a great fondness for inventing gods, and this will not disappear as knowledge advances and the need for supernatural explanations diminishes. "The history of the world tells you that I shall do this, that all men will do it. By which of your laws are you going to lay all the devilish conceptions of God which will soon be let loose on the world?" (*Religio*, 17). Is not the Christian conception much better?

About a third of the way into the tract, Hughes acknowledges that his argument up to that point has been speculative and negative rather than concrete and positive, and announces, in the kind of direct appeal to his readers to which he resorts throughout, that its direction is about to change. "I have been speaking of that which I cannot believe; let me speak to you of that which I do believe, of that which I hold to be a faith, the faith, the only faith for mankind. Do not turn from it because it seems to be egotistic. I can only speak for myself, for what I know in my own heart and conscience" (*Religio*, 18).

As John Henry Newman, a very different and much subtler religious thinker, was to do three years later in his *Apologia pro vita sua*, Hughes bases his whole religious position on subjective certitude acquired early in life by means not entirely known or knowable. "I was bred as a child and as a boy to look upon Christ as the true and rightful King and Head of our race, the Son of God and the Son of man" (*Religio*, 18). This belief—this conviction, this "longing"—grew in Hughes's manhood and led to the unquestioning acceptance of certain corollaries. In order to fulfill his mission, it is clear that Christ "must be perfect man as well as perfect God," must "have felt our sorrows, pains, temptations, weaknesses" (*Religio*, 19)—hence Hughes's belief in the Incarnation. In order to stand as the supreme example of "perfect obedience," Christ was obliged to sacrifice himself by his Father's will so that mankind, too, would "sacrifice ourselves to Him for our brethren" (*Religio*, 20)—hence Hughes's belief in the Atonement.

It is impossible, Hughes says, for him or anyone else to know Christ except through revelation, but this is by no means limited to the Bible. On the contrary, the most important revelation of Christ is internal, "in the heart of you, and of me, and of every man and woman, who is now, or ever has been, on this earth" (*Religio*, 20). To attain this kind of revelation is not difficult; we only need to "give ourselves up to His guidance, and He will accept the trust, and guide us into the knowledge of God, and of all truth" (*Religio*, 21).

Though he deplores bibliolatry, which deludes men into worshiping "the book, and not Him of whom the book speaks" (*Religio*, 21), Hughes does regard the Bible with special affection and reverence. Modern critics may quibble about its authorship, but it is clear to Hughes "that the writers of Holy Scripture were directly inspired by God, in a manner, and to an extent, in and to which no other men whose words have come down to us have been inspired" (*Religio*, 22). Therefore, as the one best source of written revelation, "the Bible is and must remain *the* inspired Book, the Book of the Church for all time.... There may be another Homer, Plato, Shakespere; there can be no other Bible" (*Religio*, 23).

Controversies about the textual accuracy of the Bible interest Hughes as little as controversies about the precise way in which it may have been inspired. The wording of this or that biblical passage may be in dispute, but such differences among scholars take nothing away from what those passages convey. "What is all this to me? ... They have told me what I wanted to know. Burn every copy in the world to-morrow, you don't and can't take that knowledge from me, or any man" (*Religio*, 25).

As to the miracles recorded in the Bible—miracles that strike many in an age of science as incredible—Hughes is also perfectly at ease. There is no inconsistency, he argues, between a belief in miracles and a belief in natural laws. God, who presides over those laws, also has the power to suspend them, and He does not exercise that power capriciously. Indeed, those suspensions of natural laws we call miracles do God's work and contribute to God's order, often restoring "an order which had been disturbed," for example by "healing the sick" or even "raising the dead" (*Religio*, 27).

Nor, finally, is Hughes, writing within two years after the publication of Darwin's *The Origin of Species*, concerned by evolutionary theory and its challenge to the Old Testament version of creation. From Hughes's perspective as a devout layman, controversy about "cosmogonies" is irrelevant. "If all cosmogonies were to disappear tomorrow, I should be none the poorer. As nothing will make me believe that God did not create the earth, and man to rule it, no faith of mine hangs on them" (*Religio*, 28–29).

Having pitted his faith, his subjective certitude, against those who vainly attempt to chip away at religion with the tools of scholarship and science, Hughes turns next to the arguments of those who would undermine Christianity with the charge that it is a selfish or an exclusive creed, that there is something base about a "faith in which, however beautiful and noble the moral teaching may be, the ultimate appeal has always been to the hope of reward and fear of punishment" (*Religio*, 31).

In order to answer this charge, Hughes insists, one must examine the meaning of reward and punishment, not as they are defined in human pronouncements or sectarian quarrels, but rather as they appear in the teachings and example of Christ. As the result of such scrutiny, Hughes is convinced that far more is involved in Christian living than the desire to achieve eternal bliss or avoid eternal damnation in the afterlife. On the contrary, he maintains, in the Christian view reward and punishment have to do with one's relations with God and other men and women rather than with mere self-gratification. "Christ has told me that the only reward I shall ever get will be 'life eternal,' and that life eternal is to know God and Him. That is all the reward I care about. The only punishment I can bring on myself will be, to banish myself from His presence and the presence of all who know Him, to dwell apart from Him and my brethren, shut up in myself" (*Religio*, 31–32).

The kingdom of God is to be found, not after death, but in life, a life of action rather than of contemplation. Christ himself—the supreme example and driving force behind the Christian Socialist movement—was not given to "the separatist and exclusive habits and maxims" (*Religio*, 34) often ascribed, with cause, to clergymen. On the contrary, Christ insisted on involving himself with all sorts of people, not always of the most savory kind. "He who believes in Him must go into every society where he has any call whatever." Especially those who strive to ameliorate "the miseries and disorders of England and the world" (*Religio*, 35) and are prone to the discouragement to which that commitment all too often gives rise need Christ: "that light and guidance, that renewal of strength and hope, that certainty as to your side and your road" (*Religio*, 36).

The affirmation of a layman's faith that Hughes outlines in this tract may not, he concedes, survive serious critical scrutiny; but that does not concern him, for his purpose is not to persuade. Rather than anything like rigorous proof, he is offering the heartfelt testimonial of one who has experienced more than his share of frustrating labor and searing adversity that belief in Christ is a uniquely powerful source of strength. Having devoted the body of *Religio Laici* to an intensely personal statement of his subjective religious certitude, Hughes concludes on an equally personal interrogatory note, in effect asking his audience if it is not likely that the faith in Christ that has sustained him will also help others. "My younger brothers, you on whom the future of England, under God, at this moment depends, will you not try Him? Is He not worth a trial?" (*Religio*, 39).

The Old Church; What Shall We Do with It?

Seventeen years passed before Hughes again published a book setting forth his religious convictions, but during that interval he frequently spoke out in defense of the principles to which he adhered. In the 1860s and 1870s, the problem for a thoughtful and concerned believer like Hughes went beyond defining acceptable bases for one's faith in God, Christ, and the Bible: now the national Church of England in which Hughes had been raised and to which he remained strongly committed was being subjected to particularly disturbing challenges from at least three different directions.

There were, of course, the unbelievers, those who were confident that *any* religion based on revelation and tradition was badly at odds with what they took to be the state of knowledge at the time. Hughes had already attempted to deal with their arguments, and he did not greatly concern himself with them after *Religio Laici*, for in his view there were even more dangerous forces working to undermine the national church.

One of these was exerted by a group of men who were no less of a threat because they were themselves ardent Christians: not members of the Anglican church, however, but of one or another of the dissenting or nonconformist Protestant sects. By mid-century, they had come to feel that it was grossly unfair for the established church and its adherents to go on monopolizing the privileged position that had been theirs, with some interruptions, since the reign of Henry VIII, and accordingly they advocated the disestablishment of the Church of England: that is, stripping it of the revenues, the rights, and the immunities that grew out of its intimate connection with the sources of secular power in the country. It will be convenient to refer to these men by the term that Hughes himself applied to them, liberationists, after the name of their most powerful organization, the Society for the Liberation of Religion from State Patronage and Control.

In the House of Commons and on lecture platforms, Hughes spoke out against legislation that would lead to the separation of church and state in England,[9] maintaining that the only way to foil the liberationists and save the national church was to reform that institution. Though Hughes's speeches drew wide support, they also brought down much wrath on his head. On the one hand, many of his allies in the cooperative and trade-union movements were outraged at his associating himself with certain Conservative M.P.s in taking the positions he did; on the other hand, a number of orthodox churchmen were appalled by what they saw as the radicalism of some of the departures from Anglican tradition for which Hughes pressed in his desire to make the Church of England acceptable to those Protestants who had refused to join it for one reason or another.

Another threat to the continuing existence of the national church actually came from within the Church of England: from the so-called ritualists, spiritual offshoots of the later stages of the Oxford Movement who advocated a return to medieval ceremonial practices more closely associated with Roman Catholicism than with Anglicanism. Ritualism was perceived as a grave danger, not least because many ritualists were quite prepared to cut the church's ties with the state in order to gain greater freedom to profess their beliefs and carry out their rites.

Hughes, whose attitude toward the original Oxford Movement was at best ambivalent from his years at Oriel College on, had taken a stand against what he considered the excesses of ritualism as early as 1860, when a controversy that had been growing in intensity for some time over the Anglo-Catholic practices of the Reverend Bryan King, rector of the slum parish of St. George's-in-the-East in London's dockland, erupted into frequent rioting in King's church. Lesser measures having failed, the Bishop of London reluctantly came to the conclusion that there would be no end to mob violence in the parish so long as King remained in his post; and, on Hughes's advice, he installed Hughes's old friend and fellow-Christian Socialist the Reverend Septimus Hansard at St. George's. In Hughes's view, there should be no trifling with the ritualists' unwillingness to submit themselves to duly constituted authority, and he held that the established church's temporizing in the face of what he called "all this millinery business" had led directly to the scandalous scenes at St. George's-in-the-East.[10] By the 1870s, Hughes had come to regard the ritualists as defiant and dangerous troublemakers.

When *The Old Church; What Shall We Do with It?* was published in 1878, it offered nothing new. Rather, the book restates views that Hughes had been expressing orally for nearly twenty years, and in fact most of it consists of the texts of speeches he had delivered on various occasions before very different audiences. Largely for that reason, its argument—unlike that of *Religio Laici* or of Hughes's next book, *The Manliness of Christ*—does not move through clearly defined stages; it is repetitious and, seemingly at least, not always quite consistent. A clear antiliberationist, antiritualist thesis does, however, emerge from *The Old Church*: the preservation of the Church establishment is essential to the well-being of the country, but the national church cannot survive unless it undergoes changes that would broaden its appeal to all English Christians.

One troubling feature of *The Old Church* is that it reveals what appears to be some ambivalence in Hughes's attitude toward the Church of England. He praises it for its comprehensiveness and openness to new ideas, but he also admonishes it for its adherence to doctrines and practices that have aroused considerable aversion among non-Anglicans. Hughes attempts to clarify his position by pointing out that the church should not be equated with the clergy. The Church of England—and this is its great strength as a *national* institution—is the creation of the people, not something imposed on them: "it is they who have the ultimate control over it, they govern it through and by the same machinery which they use for carrying on their civil business."[11] Expressing the national character and the popular will in this way, the church is liberal, tolerant, and democratic. By contrast, the clergy tends to be conservative, hostile to new thought, and anxious to keep aloof "from the nation in general, and particularly from . . . their Nonconformist brethren" (*Church*, 206).

According to Hughes, one of the glories of the Anglican establishment is that in any contest between the church (as he defines it) and the clergy, the church will sooner or later emerge victorious and carry the clergy along with it. In support of this contention, Hughes cites the history of the *Essays and Reviews* controversy: though the book and its authors were initially condemned by the clergy, they were ultimately vindicated by the church, which is to say the nation;

now, less than two decades later, "orthodox popular preachers" are proclaiming from their pulpits ideas "which are quite abreast of anything in 'Essays and Reviews,' but excite scarcely a murmur or remonstrance even in religious newspapers" (*Church*, 174). If one takes the long view, as Hughes urges, it becomes clear that such internal rifts are normally not permanent. Based as it is on the principle of "inclusiveness," embracing many different shades of opinion, a national church is better able to accommodate dissent, and less likely to split into sects over relatively minor issues, than are the "voluntary Churches" (i.e., the independent Protestant denominations), which were founded in a spirit of "exclusiveness" (*Church*, 93).

It is no accident that the broadly based Church of England is at least relatively progressive, for, Hughes maintains, "all State Churches are liberal, and . . . all voluntary Churches are illiberal" by their very natures. This is true even in the Roman Catholic Church as it exists on different terms in different countries. During the debates that were carried on in the 1860s regarding the dogma of papal infallibility, for example, "the members of the State Church of Germany, the members of the State Church of Hungary, the members of the State Church of France" expressed their opposition to the idea, which Hughes deplores as not only "illiberal" but "monstrous," whereas "the voluntary Romish Church of England, the voluntary Romish Church of Ireland, the voluntary Romish Church of America" favored it (*Church*, 73). As to American Christianity in general, Hughes devotes the fifth chapter of *The Old Church* to an examination of what he calls "The Great Experiment of the Pure Voluntary System" in the United States and concludes that the separation of church and state has failed to achieve the ends envisioned by American ideologues—that, in fact, the lack of a church establishment in this country has led to more narrow-mindedness and friction in the religious sphere and more spiritual impoverishment in public life generally than would be tolerated in England.

Only a truly national institution like the Church of England, whose representatives are to be found in every single parish of the country, can make its services available to all, without cost or obligation, especially to those who need them most—the indigent, the outcast, and the remotely situated. Indeed, every Englishman and Englishwoman has access to these services as a "birthright" (*Church*, 92).

No one is required to use them, of course, and their provision is entirely consistent with complete freedom to worship as one pleases, or not to worship at all.

Some of the other advantages of a national church may appear to be largely symbolic, but in Hughes's judgment that does not make them less significant or less real. For instance, the continuing existence of the Church of England attests to "the fact that the nation in its corporate capacity has a spiritual as well as a material life; that it cannot, even if it would, confine itself to the preservation of material things, of body and goods" (*Church*, 28). The traditional union of church and state in England thus articulates and reinforces a desirably comprehensive view of what is important in human existence.

It is not only in the spiritual realm that the national church has enriched the life of England; it has also been a potent force for good in the realm of the mind and that of the imagination. In the study of history, in moral philosophy and metaphysics, in what Hughes calls "general literature"—in all these fields of endeavor, churchmen have distinguished themselves, whereas nonconformists have made virtually no contribution. This is so because members of the Church of England carry on their speculations in a bracing atmosphere from which the nonconformists have cut themselves off—a "freer atmosphere" (*Church*, 57) that arises from the close relationship between the whole nation and the church.

Whatever the liberationists or the ritualists say, then, Hughes contends that the Church of England has yielded innumerable benefits, and these would diminish or disappear altogether if it were disestablished. In that unhappy event, a broad liberal institution would be replaced by narrow conservative sects; religious tolerance would give way to factional strife; the people would lose most of the practical advantages provided by the church; the life of the country would become increasingly materialistic and secular; and significant intellectual and imaginative activity would be discouraged.

According to Hughes, the way to defend the church against its adversaries is not to destroy it by disestablishment, but rather to reform it: to make the church truly national, "wide enough to include all English Christians who own no human allegiance outside their own nation" (*Church*, 16). The barriers that have kept many of them out should be removed, and this can be done without giving up any of the church's fundamental attributes. Precisely because it is a national establishment, the Church of England can be changed in such ways in harmony with the will of the people, through legislative action.

If the Acts of Uniformity, which spell out the special status of the Book of Common Prayer in the Church of England, constitute a barrier, they can be repealed. If the requirement that Anglican clergy subscribe to the Thirty-Nine Articles, which set forth the basic tenets of the Church of England, constitutes a barrier, it can be modified. If the inclusion in the Book of Common Prayer of the Athanasian Creed, which condemns to everlasting damnation those who do not "hold the Catholic faith," constitutes a barrier, it can be eliminated. "Other modifications in the rubrics and Common prayer would be necessary, upon the liberal and Christian principle of avoiding offence wherever this can be done without abandoning essentials, or violating principles" (*Church*, 18).

Organizational problems, too, need correction if non-Anglican Protestants are to be won over to the Church of England. Hughes lists and briefly discusses some of these "anomalies which exist inside the Church" and which "it should be the object of every good Churchman to reform" (*Church*, 33) with a view to making the church more representative of and more responsive to the people of the nation. First, Convocation—i.e., the assemblies of the provinces of Canterbury and York—should be reconstituted so as to lessen the power of "deans, archdeacons, and other *ex officio* members" (*Church*, 34) and "to secure a more adequate representation of the Church" (*Church*, 24). Second, the laity of each parish should have more of a voice in church affairs. Third, "the sale of benefices, the great scandal of our Church" (*Church*, 34), should be abolished. Fourth, a new method of appointing bishops should be devised. Fifth, cathedral endowments should be used "to a greater extent for some spiritual and practical work in harmony with the parochial system" (*Church*, 35). And, sixth, small parishes should be amalgamated so as to provide both sufficient income and sufficient work for clergymen.

Hughes concedes that, no matter how thoroughly the establishment is reformed, there will always be nonconformists who will wish to stay outside the national church. The way to deal with them is not as adversaries but as brothers and sisters in Christ, men and women who would have remained "in the same communion, as they were in the Tudor times," except for "mischievous" legislation like the Acts of Uniformity (*Church*, 30–31). But what has been done by laws can, to a great extent, be undone by laws. In fact, a great deal of this work of reconciliation has already been accomplished, beginning with the repeal of the Test and Corporation Acts, which excluded nonconformists from Parliament, in 1828, fifty years before the publication of *The Old Church*. More remains to be done, however: for example, nonconformists "cannot bury their dead with their own services in the parochial graveyards" (*Church*, 32), and this galling condition can rather easily be remedied by the enactment of appropriate legislation.

Anglicans, Hughes suggests, should view dissenters as A. P. Stanley does, as " 'non-conforming members of the Church of England' " (*Church*, 31), and extend to them every possible courtesy. "The spirit of a national Church should not be one of jealous exclusiveness, and the best traditions of ours are in favour of hospitality. . . . We should hail with pleasure the restoration of the old liberty (for instance) of throwing open Church pulpits to persons not in Anglican orders" (*Church*, 17–18). Since most church buildings are not now fully utilized, why not, Hughes asks, make them available to nonconformists at appropriate times for appropriate purposes, including worship?

The Old Church, as we have seen, is a layman's straightforward, uncomplicated plea for reform in the English church and reconciliation among English Protestants. It is possible to argue that it is sometimes muddled and more often impractical, but there can be no doubt about the depth of feeling with which Hughes insists that such reform and reconciliation are not only good in themselves but also means to the essential end of preserving and strengthening the church establishment as a national institution.

The Manliness of Christ

Hughes's third book on religious matters grew out of a series of lectures he delivered in 1876 at the London Working Men's College. His subject was the life of Jesus, and his aim was to persuade his listeners of the applicability of much in that life to their own everyday concerns. Recondite biblical exegesis would have been inappropriate for that audience as well as foreign to the bent of Hughes's own mind, and Hughes was characteristically untroubled by the difficulties that nineteenth-century biblical criticism had put in the way of anyone who tried to piece together a totally coherent narrative of Christ's career from the evidence contained in the Gospels: "the general outline comes out clearly enough, and this is all we need in order to pursue our own particular inquiry satisfactorily."[12] An aloof and ascetic Jesus would have held no interest for the urban workmen whom Hughes was trying to reach, and accordingly he went to some pains to depict Christ as a man of the people, struggling against historical forces that were just as inexorable as those they faced eighteen and a half centuries later.

At the same time, aware that *The Manliness of Christ* was also addressed to a wider public, Hughes was anxious to correct the mistaken view of "muscular Christianity" that had been accepted by many ever since the publication of *Tom Brown's School Days.*[13] Therefore, the introduction and the first two parts, comprising about a quarter of the book, are given over to an explanation of what Hughes really means by manliness and of how this concept relates to the life of Christ and the nature of the religion he founded.

Certainly the popular notion that Christianity involves passivity and withdrawal from the world is utterly at variance with the precepts and the example of Christ as Hughes the social activist views them. Far from preaching a faith that appeals "to men's fears—to that in them which is timid and shrinking, rather than to that which is courageous and outspoken" (*Christ*, 5), Christ urged mankind toward perfection; and "constant contact and conflict with evil of all kinds," which requires "courage or manfulness," is "the necessary condition of that moral effort" (*Christ*, 7). As Hughes points out, Jesus knew this from bitter experience, for he himself was up against incredible difficulties during the three years of his ministry.

Before launching into his chronological account of Christ's career, Hughes devotes some twenty pages to defining manliness and differentiating it from courage, a term with which it is often confused. Including as it does such ingredients as "tenderness, and thoughtfulness for others" (*Christ*, 21), manliness is distinctively human, though it does demonstrate that mankind at its best both reflects and aspires to divinity. Ordinary physical courage, on the other hand, admirable and necessary though it may be at times as an ingredient or accompaniment of manliness, is really "an animal quality" (*Christ*, 22). As for the "athleticism" with which Hughes has so often been identified, it has no place in the present discussion; for, unlike manliness, it can be turned to vicious uses: "a great athlete may be a brute or a coward, while a truly manly man can be neither" (*Christ*, 26). Having sorted this much out, Hughes goes on to list three ways in which true manliness, in Christ or in ordinary mortals, goes beyond courage.

The first is the readiness to bear pain or even death for the sake of one's fellow-humans. Hughes's favorite example of "the sublimity of self-sacrifice" (*Christ*, 32) is what happened during the sinking of the *Birkenhead*, a troop ship, in the South Atlantic in 1852, when "four hundred men, at the call of their heroic officers . . . calmly and without a murmur accepted death in a horrible form rather than endanger the women and children saved in the boats" (*Christ*, 29).[14] What made this act of self-sacrifice sublime for Hughes was that the men did nothing to save themselves, demonstrating his point that "in the face of danger self-restraint is after all the highest form of self-assertion, and a characteristic of manliness as distinguished from courage" (*Christ*, 33).

The second attribute of manliness is unswerving loyalty to truth, which is, according to Hughes, "the most rare and difficult of all human qualities" (*Christ*, 34–35). It is easy to bear witness to truth when it is in open conflict with falsehood, when truth is popular and falsehood is not. "But to bear it against those we love, against those whose judgment and opinions we respect, in defence or further-ance of that which approves itself as true to our own inmost con-science, this is the last and abiding test of courage and of manli-ness" (*Christ*, 35).

Finally, manliness is marked by the subordination of the human will to one's sense of duty: duty to one's leaders, and ultimately duty to one's God. Here Hughes cites the account by the Roman historian Tacitus of Julius Atticus's murder of Otho, the rival of his chief, Galba; when Julius Atticus tells Galba what he has done, expecting to be praised for it, Galba's disapproving rejoinder is noth-ing more than " 'My comrade, by whose order?' " (*Christ*, 38). Julius Atticus's duty, regardless of his own inclinations, was to carry out the will of Galba; Christ's duty, and ours, is " 'to do the will of my Father and your Father' " (*Christ*, 40).

When Hughes turns to the life of Jesus, he divides it into three stages: his boyhood, to which Hughes devotes part III of *The Manli-ness of Christ*; his call to the ministry, the subject of part IV; and his ministry itself, subdivided into four "Acts," which are dealt with in parts V, VI, VII, and VIII, respectively. In each of these six sections, Hughes is much less concerned with biographical facts than he is with showing how Christ's exalted manliness can be inferred from what is known about him.

There is very little information about the boyhood of Jesus in the Gospels. We have only Luke's account of the twelve-year-old child's visit to the temple at Jerusalem, where he astonished the learned doctors by the questions he asked and the answers he gave. To his mother's reproach that he had caused his parents concern by slipping away from them—"thy father and I have sought thee sorrowing"— Jesus replied, "How is it that ye sought me? wist ye not that I must be about my Father's business?" (Luke 2:49).

Though it is all he has to work with from that period of Christ's life, Hughes nevertheless uses this remarkable incident to support the case he is making as to the character and significance of Jesus. Aided by "Mr. Holman Hunt's great picture" (*Christ*, 44) of *The Finding of the Saviour in the Temple*, Hughes draws three conclusions about what Christ's encounter with the rabbis shows. First, even before this journey to Jerusalem, Jesus must have been aware that he was somehow set apart. Second, his conversation with the doctors must have strengthened this dawning awareness of his difference from others. Third, after his return to Nazareth with Mary and Joseph, Christ's consciousness of his unique destiny, perhaps even as the Messiah whom his people were awaiting so eagerly, must have continued to grow within him. And yet, despite its ever-increasing urgency, this sense of mission remained internal, and Jesus did not speak out in the synagogue at Nazareth until the age of thirty, having been baptized by John and assured by the Holy Spirit that he was indeed the son of God.

For Hughes, this eighteen-year silence of Christ's is irrefutable proof of his manliness. Jesus must have spent that long interval perfecting himself, "making Himself all that God had meant Him to be," and awaiting the call that would "convince Him that the voice within has not been a lying voice" (*Christ*, 60). It is unreasonable to assume that as a boy, as a youth, and as an adult Jesus could have been free from the temptations that occur at those stages of life, but his unyielding response to the devil's blandishments during the forty days he spent in the wilderness after his baptism demonstrates that he must have learned how to rise "clear above them through the strength of perfect obedience, the strength which comes from the daily fulfilment of daily duties" (*Christ*, 50). Such obedience to the will of God under great difficulties is an important characteristic of manliness, and so is Christ's self-restraint. Even though aware from boyhood that he possessed miraculous powers growing out of his being "more perfectly in sympathy with God's creation than any mediaeval saint, or modern naturalist, or man of science" (*Christ*, 66), Jesus was able to refrain from exercising them until the call finally came.

Hughes finds further indications of the manliness of Jesus in his response to that call. He surmises that Christ, like many Judeans when they first heard about John the Baptist's announcement that the kingdom of heaven was at hand, initially assumed that John himself was the Messiah. "May we not also fairly conjecture that, on His way to Betharaba, to claim his place in the national confession and uprising, He must have had moments of rejoicing that the chief part in the great drama seemed likely after all to be laid on another? As a rule, the more thoroughly disciplined and fit a man may be for any really great work, the more conscious will he be of his own unfitness for it, the more distrustful of himself, the more anxious not to thrust himself forward" (*Christ*, 73).

When informed that he and not John is in fact "the Lamb of God" (John 1:29), Jesus withdraws into the wilderness to fast and meditate, "to wrestle with, and master, the tremendous disclosure" (*Christ*, 78). For Hughes, the significance of those forty days rests not so much in Christ's skillful rebuffs of Satan, recorded by Matthew and Luke, as in his finally coming to terms with the nature of his own mission, which is not to follow his own bent but rather to do God's bidding. It has taken Christ thirty years to achieve such total awareness, and at the end of part IV Hughes comments that this shows that the most important characteristic to be noted in Christ's life up to that point is "patience—a resolute waiting on God's mind," which constitutes "the highest ideal we can form of human conduct," "the noblest type of true manliness" (*Christ*, 85).

Once Christ assumes his ministry, he repeatedly demonstrates not only great physical courage but also a manliness that is literally exemplary. He unfailingly upholds the truth, even though this is sometimes very difficult for him. When, for example, he preaches in the synagogue at Nazareth, he knows that his words will inevitably entail "the bitter pain of alienating those whom He loved and respected . . . but who could not for the time rise out of the conventional, respectable, way of looking at things" (*Christ*, 108). For

Christ there can be no "bending to expediency, or forgetting the means in the end. He never for one moment accommodates His life or teaching to any standard but the highest" (*Christ*, 113), holding steadfastly to his course regardless of the consequences.

Among those he offends by his forthrightness are not only many of his own followers but also the most powerful rulers of his people, and by the summer of the second year of his ministry it has become clear to him that the redemption of mankind will require "His own perfect and absolute sacrifice and humiliation." But even Christ's ultimate self-sacrifice requires a manly self-restraint: he must choose the appropriate place, await the appropriate moment, to undergo his suffering and death. "This must be done at Jerusalem, the centre of the national life and the seat of the Roman Government. It must be done during the Passover, the national commemoration of sacrifice and deliverance" (*Christ*, 130).

As Christ's ministry draws to a close and he is about to be arrested and tried, he retires with his disciples to the Garden of Gethsemane, where he displays unmistakable symptoms of agitation. Can the view of Christ as manly, Hughes asks, be reconciled with "such signs of physical fear and weakness" (*Christ*, 144) in the face of danger? Answering in the affirmative, Hughes makes two points: what really lacerates Jesus at this dreadful time is not fear and weakness so much as it is the "sense of utter loneliness" (*Christ*, 148) that comes from being abandoned by all his earthly associates, a sense that is confirmed when his disciples fall asleep despite his plea that they keep vigil with him; and, in view of what follows this episode, there can be no question about the sublime manliness of Jesus, for the real test occurs "when the danger comes, not when he is in solitary preparation for it" (*Christ*, 149).

The Jesus depicted by Thomas Hughes in *The Manliness of Christ*, then, is not the founder of "muscular Christianity" as it has been caricatured since the middle of the nineteenth century. Rather than mere physical prowess, he exhibits in the highest degree those vital moral and spiritual qualities that comprise manliness properly defined, and his life continues in Hughes's day to serve as an inspiration and a model to men and women as they go about their work, however humble it may be, as citizens and as Christians.

Chapter Four

Writings about America

Hughes's attitudes toward the momentous events that were occurring in the United States before and during the Civil War were deeply colored by the same Christian commitment that marked his other work of the 1850s and early 1860s. What may be less obvious is that even after the emancipation of the slaves and the cessation of hostilities his continuing interest in America grew out of religious, social, and political convictions that also found expression in his writings about his own country.

Slavery and the American Civil War

Three pieces of printed prose best exemplify Hughes's hatred of slavery and his advocacy of the Northern cause in the years before 1865: "Opinion on American Affairs" (1861), an article cast as a lengthy letter to the editor of *Macmillan's Magazine*; "The Struggle for Kansas" (1862), a sixty-two-page supplement to Ludlow's *A Sketch of the History of the United States*; and *The Cause of Freedom: Which Is Its Champion in America, The North or the South?* (1863), a pamphlet divided equally between the text of an important speech and some "Introductory Remarks" that expand on what he had said orally. They are of interest not only for the views they espouse but also for the mode of argument that Hughes employed.

"**Opinion on American Affairs.**" When news of the Confederate triumph in the first Battle of Bull Run, the initial major engagement of the Civil War, reached England in August 1861, Hughes was on holiday at the Norfolk fishing village of Cromer. Even in this placid setting, he felt compelled to set down his own reaction because "all our leading journals . . . with the single exception of the *Spectator*" had been taking an unseemly delight in the rout of the Union army.[1] The resulting "Opinion on American Affairs" was Hughes's first published pronouncement on the Civil War; in it, he made a number of points that were to recur in his writings during the next four years.

First, Hughes insists that the widespread derision with which the outcome of the battle was greeted by significant organs of opinion in his country has "been ungenerous and unfair, and has not represented the better mind of England" ("Opinion," 414). The North had not been prepared for war. Nevertheless, when the Union's patient hopes for some sort of "amicable arrangement" with the seceding states finally proved unfounded, "at the word of the President the whole North rose as one man" in "as grand, as noble, a national act, as any which we have seen, or are likely to see, in our generation" ("Opinion," 415), and the English people approved and admired the Northern resolve. Hughes never tired of pointing out to his audiences, first in England and later in the United States, that the establishment press and establishment politicians did not necessarily speak for the nation in their utterances on the Civil War.

Hughes grants that there had indeed been instances of dereliction of duty and panic on the Northern side, as English journalists rather smugly reported, but he points out that many of these troops "had been hastily thrown together, and half drilled" ("Opinion," 415) and that the general standard of conduct in General McDowell's army had been at least as high as one had any right to expect given the circumstances under which it fought at Bull Run. He reminds his readers that the Northern command had yielded to political and journalistic pressures in committing its troops to battle and attempting to advance on Richmond, the Confederate capital, before the men were properly trained. The press, particularly the English press, cannot be trusted to write responsibly of affairs about which it knows nothing. "On the news of the defeat, all the best of the Northern papers have acknowledged their error, and formally undertaken to refrain from military criticism. Our own papers are so little in the habit of acknowledging themselves in the wrong, or of abstaining from criticism, however ill-judged, on any matter under the sun, that I confess to being rather struck by this action of the American journalists" ("Opinion," 416).

By the late summer of 1861, relations between England and the Union were in a sorry state. Britain had declared her neutrality in the Civil War. Though there was virtually no proslavery sentiment and the government had refrained from recognizing the Confederacy, there was also very little support in England for the idea of keeping the American Union together by force of arms. Many in the North found the English position incomprehensible, and the New York press made things worse by attributing it to "low material considerations," "base selfishness," and "canting hypocrisy."[2] As Hughes notes, these fantasies of unscrupulous Northern journalists were duly reported by their equally unscrupulous London counterparts. The result of all this irresponsible scribbling was an exacerbation of feelings on the English side, and this doubtless had some bearing on the way the news from Virginia was received. Interrupting his summer vacation to write to *Macmillan's* on a matter that concerned him deeply, Hughes assumed a role he was to play on many more formal occasions during the next two decades: that of the man in the middle, trying to bring about better Anglo-American understanding by urging each nation to judge the other at its best and not at its worst. "I quite admit that the tone of the Government and people of the North has been such as deeply to grieve and disappoint every right-minded Englishman; but don't let us saddle them with the frantic slanders of the *New York Herald*" ("Opinion," 416).

But Hughes's fundamental point in the article is that one must look beyond the shifts in the fortunes of war and the resulting shifts in the tides of public opinion to the principle that is at stake in this conflict. "If the North were right before, they are right now, though defeated" ("Opinion," 415). That they were, and are, right—that they are engaged in a fight against slavery and for freedom, which is God's fight—there is no doubt whatever in Hughes's mind. If the North is defeated in that fight, "it will be a misfortune such as has not come on the world since Christendom arose," "the greatest misfortune which can happen to us and to mankind." Therefore, "God grant that they may hold on, and be strong! God grant that they may remember that the greatest triumphs have always come, and must always come, to men through the greatest humiliations" ("Opinion," 416).

"The Struggle for Kansas."   During the late summer and autumn of 1861, J. M. Ludlow delivered a series of lectures on American history at the London Working Men's College. When these were published by Macmillan the next year as *A Sketch of the History of the United States*, the volume also contained Hughes's "The Struggle for Kansas," which was based on two lectures he had given to the same audience after Ludlow had concluded his.

This joining of Hughes's work to Ludlow's in one book was highly appropriate. Both of them were much less interested in detailing historical facts, dates, and personalities than they were in expounding a point of view about the direction that American history had taken from Colonial times to Secession. In their judgment as religious men who had agreed ever since their collaboration in the Christian Socialist movement on the supreme importance of applying the Gospel to political and social questions, slavery was immoral and contrary to the teachings of Jesus. They saw the Civil War, which was still in its first year, as a climactic contest in which that evil of long standing would surely be expunged, and the will of God would inevitably prevail in the victory of the North.

In launching into "The Struggle for Kansas," Hughes is quite explicit about his partisanship and the reason for it. "I hate slavery of every kind,—of the body, of the intellect, of the spirit,—with a perfect hatred. I believe it to be the will of God that all men should be free, and that Christ came into the world to do God's will, and to break *every* yoke."[3] The "struggle" in Kansas from its organization as a territory in 1854 until its admission to the Union as a state in January 1861 had been between the free-soilers and the proponents of slavery, and Hughes makes it plain from the outset that all his sympathies lie with the former, though he insists that he will base his argument on facts, suppressing none that might damage his case.

Why devote well over 20 percent of a book dealing with the history of the United States to the agony of a single territory during the seven bloody years it took to achieve statehood? In Hughes's view, Kansas had been a microcosm of the whole American republic, its "struggle" not only foreshadowing the issues of that much vaster "struggle which is now raging," but also illustrating "remarkably the strength and the weakness of the great nation engaged in that struggle" ("Struggle," 322). Though far from democratic, the government of the United States throughout the first eight decades of the nation's existence had been reasonably responsive to the will of the electorate, such as it was. This was a strength. That the electorate did not always act from the highest motives and that the conflicting interests of its component segments could be reconciled, if at all, only through political maneuvering and not on principle was a grave weakness.

Never in American history did this weakness lead to more lamentable results than in the matter of slavery, specifically with regard

to the perceived need to maintain some kind of balance between the
number of free states and the number of slave states in the Union.
Though he might have gone back even farther, Hughes discerns the
origins of the troubles of Kansas in the Missouri Compromise of
1820, by which, after weeks of wrangling, Congress finally agreed
to admit Missouri as a slave state, and Maine as a free state, on the
explicit understanding that slavery would be excluded from the rest
of the Louisiana Purchase north of 36° 30'. Whatever the political
advantages of this disposition of such a huge stretch of land between
the Mississippi and the Rocky Mountains might have been, it ignored
the will of "the Lord of the whole earth," and, in Hughes's judgment,
that was a fatal flaw: "one of the lessons which stand out in letters
of sunlight on the face of History is, that He is against all such
compromises,—that He will allow no system of wrong or robbery
to be fixed on any part of His earth" ("Struggle," 323). Any attempt
to reach a compromise between good and evil is doomed to fail
sooner or later—not only because of God's displeasure with it, but
also because of the deviousness and rascality of the forces of evil,
which will lead them to violate its terms. As Hosea Biglow points
out in a line of Lowell's of which Hughes was especially fond:
"Conciliate? it jest means *be kicked.*"[4]

And indeed the Missouri Compromise did not remain "fixed" much
longer than a single generation. The Kansas-Nebraska Act of 1854,
rather than barring slavery from those territories as the Missouri
Compromise had guaranteed, provided for "popular sovereignty,"
leaving it up to the people of each territory to determine on what
basis they would organize their system. To the dismay of such United
States senators as Charles Sumner and Salmon P. Chase at the time,
and of Thomas Hughes later, this piece of legislation totally dis-
regarded the principled arguments against slavery.

Worse than that, at least as far as the Kansas Territory was concerned, it led to a period during which each side tried by all means
at its command to gain control of the territorial government so that
it might make its views on the slavery question prevail. Hughes's
characterizations of the contending parties make it clear which has his
sympathy. The proslavery men, he remarks, had found it easy to
cross over to Kansas from the neighboring slave state of Missouri. A
considerable number of them came only to harass their adversaries
and vote in elections, returning home when their missions were

accomplished. The free-soilers, by contrast, were genuine settlers, often sponsored by high-minded emigrant aid societies as far away as New England. They were "very unlike the usual coon-hunting, whisky-drinking pioneers of the West," but rather "educated and intelligent men" who "brought with them not only civilised habits, but saw-mills, capital, and other material aid" ("Struggle," 329).

Hughes devotes some fifty pages of "The Struggle for Kansas" to a circumstantial account of the contest that afflicted the territory following passage of the Kansas-Nebraska Act, a contest whose nature is well indicated by the term "Bleeding Kansas," which was often used by journalists and politicians during the 1850s.[5] Virtually from the start, the free-soilers enjoyed a numerical majority, but, as Hughes tells the story, their forbearance and high-mindedness put them at a disadvantage against the fraud and violence to which the proslavery side habitually resorted. Each party convened its own legislature and drew up its own constitution, so that it was difficult to tell, especially from some distance, who was actually in charge in Kansas.

Certainly in Washington the Kansas free-soilers received little understanding and less support. Two successive presidents paid no attention to their claims that they and not the intruders from Missouri represented "popular sovereignty" in the territory. When the Topeka legislature applied for the admission of Kansas as a free state in 1855, President Pierce came out in opposition, "declaring that the people of Kansas had no right to organise as a state without a previous enabling Act of Congress" ("Struggle," 344). Even after the people endorsed the Topeka constitution at the polls, Pierce remained unmoved, "sanctioning the territorial (bogus) legislature which had been elected by the Missouri invaders, and declaring that the territorial (bogus) laws would be sustained by the whole force of the Government" ("Struggle," 350). Federal troops from Fort Leavenworth, acting under Pierce's orders, dispersed the free-state legislature when it attempted to hold its first scheduled meeting on July 4, 1856. James Buchanan, who succeeded Pierce in the presidency in 1857, did not look any more kindly on the free-soilers than his predecessor had. Though it should have been abundantly clear by then that the prevailing sentiment in Kansas was hostile to slavery, Buchanan accepted the proslavery Lecompton constitution, which had not been ratified by the voters, rather than the free-state

Topeka one, which had. When the acting governor, Frederick P. Stanton, convened the legally elected legislature, Buchanan dismissed him.

All the considerable power of the executive branch of the federal government was thus arrayed against the opponents of slavery in the Kansas Territory. So was the judiciary: United States District Court Judge Samuel D. Lecompte was an ardent proslavery man and frequently ruled against the free-soilers. As to the United States Congress, only after years of debate that had little to do with the moral principles at issue did it finally approve the admission of Kansas as a free state in January 1861—less than a year before Hughes lectured to the London workmen on this subject.

Despite such hostility and indifference in Washington, and a great deal of chicanery and brute force close to home, the antislavery cause in Kansas did prevail, giving the lie to the old saw that might makes right. In God's world, Hughes insists, that cannot be so, certainly not in the long run. Shortly after "the free-state settlers of Kansas had reached the lowest point of their humiliation" ("Struggle," 363) in July 1856, when a United States Army contingent prevented the Topeka legislature from meeting, the tide began to turn in their favor. Though sporadic guerrilla warfare continued, by the end of that year there was no doubt that they would win.

Long before the achievement of statehood and the start of the Civil War in 1861, "the struggle for Kansas" had served a salutary purpose. "The border ruffian bands had failed in their special object, but had effected much, for they had opened the eyes of the North to the meaning of 'squatter sovereignty' in the territories in Southern mouths; they had converted thousands of Democrats in Kansas and Missouri into free soilers; they had proved the truth of [Senator William H.] Seward's words, that compromise between freedom and slavery was thenceforth impossible, and had opened the great contest" ("Struggle," 367).

Not only was this struggle "the beginning of the present war" ("Struggle," 378), but it also helped to define the terms according to which the conflict would be waged. The Democratic party split over the proslavery Lecompton constitution "when [Senator Stephen A.] Douglas ratted" ("Struggle," 379), unable to reconcile that document with his advocacy of "popular sovereignty"; this internal division led to the election of the Republican Abraham Lincoln in 1860.[6] The platform on which Lincoln ran and won, calling for "the limitation of slavery, the deliverance of all the remaining territories from the curse which had cost Kansas four years' war" ("Struggle," 379), would not have been so widely accepted in the North had it not been for the somber lessons of "the struggle for Kansas."

It must be said to Hughes's credit that, despite his strong anti-slavery feeling, he is not blind to the faults of the free-soilers. They were no more respectful of the rights of the Indians than the pro-slavery party was ("Struggle," 330). Their Topeka constitution contained an article, "commonly known as the 'black law,' by which coloured people were excluded from the territory" ("Struggle," 342). This was weakened in the Wyandotte state constitution of 1859 into a provision that "disfranchised the resident coloured people" ("Struggle," 376), in Hughes's eyes a deplorable failure "to be thoroughly generous and liberal" ("Struggle," 377). They occasionally committed atrocities, like the so-called Pottawatomie Massacre, but these were exceptional cases, occurring after severe provocation by the border ruffians.

Despite such serious blemishes, however, to a Christian like Hughes the cause of the Kansas free-soilers was undeniably just and that of the proslavery forces was undeniably evil. In this important respect, Hughes points out, "the struggle for Kansas" was exactly like the much greater struggle that is now raging. During the 1850s there was a great deal of pious talk in the United States about "popular sovereignty," but this was largely a smokescreen intended to obscure the moral issue at stake in Kansas. In 1861 the skillful propaganda of Confederate agents and their domestic supporters seeks to persuade the English, who are already indignant about such affronts as the Morrill tariff and the *Trent* affair, that the American Civil War is basically an economic and social conflict. Like Ludlow in his *History*, Hughes urges his compatriots to reject such specious arguments: the truth is that "the Confederate states have seceded because they found that the North would no longer permit the extension of slavery in the territories of the United States" ("Struggle," 379–80) and that the result of a Southern victory would be the perpetuation of that institution, which almost everyone in Hughes's English audience agrees in regarding as a sin before God and a crime against humanity.

The Cause of Freedom. However cogent and eloquent the arguments of Northern sympathizers like Hughes and Ludlow may have been, an influential school of thought in England continued to hold that slavery was not the main issue in the American Civil War and that it was the Union rather than the Confederacy that was trampling on liberty. On January 19, 1863, for example, an editorial in the *Times* made precisely these points. After chiding the North for the insincerity of its professed views about slavery, the writer declared "that, hating slavery, but being all unmoved by the stage tricks of Mr. LINCOLN and his friends in this matter, we look upon the American contest as a purely political quarrel, and tacitly hold our opinion that, as the cause of Italy against Austria is the cause of freedom, so also the cause of the South gallantly defending itself against the cruel and desolating invasion of the North is the cause of freedom."[7]

This editorial gave Hughes the text for a speech that he delivered ten days later before a large and enthusiastic meeting sponsored by the London Emancipation Society. Hughes insisted that, far from defending "the cause of freedom" as the *Times* argued, the Confederacy is fighting for "the cause of the most degrading and hateful slavery that has been before the world for thousands of years."[8]

Look at the leadership of the South, Hughes suggests to his audience. The blatantly proslavery and antiblack convictions of the Confederate president and vice-president, Jefferson Davis and Alexander H. Stephens, are matters of record. Particularly galling to the author of "The Struggle for Kansas" was Davis's role in that conflict of the previous decade. As Pierce's secretary of war, "he sent troops, turned out the free legislators, and had it not been for John Brown, and such men as he, slavery would have been established in Kansas by Mr. Jefferson Davis" (*Cause*, 11). As late as 1860, while serving as United States senator from Mississippi, Davis introduced a constitutional amendment that would have required all states to recognize that owning slaves was legal. As for Stephens, he is a man who asserts that the inferiority of the black race to the white is a " 'natural and normal condition' " sanctioned by God (*Cause*, 12). Another prominent Southerner well known in England, where he has been spreading Confederate propaganda for the past year, Commissioner James M. Mason, is the same politician who drafted the Fugitive Slave Act in 1850 while representing Virginia in the United States Senate.

With such leaders, how can the Confederacy possibly be advocating "the cause of freedom"? It stands for no such noble goal but only the degraded and un-Christian motives of its inhabitants. As evidence that the Southern people as a whole are (to use a term from our own age) racists, Hughes cites the dispatches of the well-known *Times* correspondent William Howard Russell. "He and all other trust-worthy witnesses describe both the people and the Government to be as deliberately hostile to freedom as any men that ever lived on the face of this earth. . . . I challenge any friend of the South to name one single leader there who is not pledged over and over again to slavery. I ask them to name one public act, one single Southern Confederate State, which is in favor of human freedom" (*Cause*, 15). Certainly the clamor in the South in favor of reopening the slave trade, prohibited by Congress more than a half-century ago, does not sound as if it comes from champions of liberty.

No matter what the editorial writer in the *Times* and like-minded Englishmen may say, then, the Confederate cause is *not* "the cause of freedom"; rather, the conclusion is inescapable that it is the cause of tyranny.

The list of speakers at Exeter Hall on that January evening in 1863 was a long one, and Hughes was allotted only twenty minutes for his address (*Cause*, 9). As delivered, therefore, the speech could not be "a full statement of the case against the Confederate States" (*Cause*, 3); instead of amending the text when it appeared in print, however, Hughes prefaced it with some "Introductory Remarks" in order to make several additional points that he was anxious to lay before his readers.

First, Hughes alludes to the deviousness and manipulativeness of the Southern leaders, their highhandedness, "their avowed designs on Mexico, Cuba, and other possessions of neighbouring powers," and their bringing about "the ever increasing degradation, morally and intellectually, of the whole black, and two-thirds of the white popula-tion of the Southern states" (*Cause*, 4). These are points that must at least be touched on if the enormity of the Confederate position is to be properly understood.

Next, he reiterates an argument he had made at the conclusion of "The Struggle for Kansas." Those Englishmen who believe that the Southern cause is "the cause of freedom" need to ask themselves what the result of a Confederate victory would be. There is ample evidence in the statements of Southern leaders to indicate that such an outcome would lead to the extension of slavery "over half a continent" (*Cause*, 6). Not only would the Union break up irre-trievably in that unhappy event, but the North American republic, except for the New England states, would turn "into a great confederacy, ruled by a fierce and proud oligarchy, and with slavery for its corner-stone. How will England like standing in a few years face to face with such a power as this?" (*Cause*, 8).

As delivered at Exeter Hall, "The Cause of Freedom" was a fighting speech. Hughes's "Introductory Remarks" do not soften the force of his spoken words, but they do serve to absolve him of the charge of demagoguery implicit in a hostile *Saturday Review* article about the Emancipation Society meeting.[9] He does not advocate fighting for its own sake now any more than he did in *Tom Brown's School Days* six years earlier. "War and bloodshed, blazing towns and villages, and starving people, are fearful sights. Every man must shrink from them, must long to see an end to them. But there are times when nations have to endure these things, when the stake at issue is so precious that the truest men and the gentlest women are the foremost to nerve their hearts to brave all miseries, to undergo all sacrifices, so that it be not lost. The present contest in America is of this kind" (*Cause*, 7).

Nor does Hughes align himself with those fiery abolitionists on both sides of the Atlantic who made freeing all the slaves the foremost of their war aims. Hughes's are much more modest. "I call any peace premature which shall not at least secure the Mississippi boundary, and shut up slavery within the Gulf States" (*Cause*, 7). A timorous abandonment of principle? Certainly not, if this statement of Hughes's is taken in the context of his whole outlook on the slavery question. Fighting as they are for this immoral institution and not for freedom, the Confederates will surely lose. God will see to that and to the ultimate destruction of slavery, which will inevitably come about once the expansionist goals of the South have been checked once and for all.

Reconciliation and Colonization

Hughes's efforts on behalf of rapprochement between his country and the United States did not end with the Civil War. Much as that conflict had deeply scarred the American body politic, it left a strong residue of ill feeling between Britain and America. To mention just one vexing dispute, the charges and countercharges over the heavy damage done to Union shipping by Confederate vessels built in British ports—the so-called *Alabama* claims—went on for years before the matter was finally settled by arbitration in 1872. During this troubled postwar era, Hughes did his best to induce each side to come to a more sympathetic grasp of the other's position.

Selected Minor Writings. In a magazine article published during the first Christmas season following the cessation of hostilities, Hughes strove to make English readers aware of how much their kinsmen in the North, and particularly in New England, had suffered and sacrificed on the long and tortuous path to victory. Whatever faults the Union might have been guilty of, its society had been transfigured by this ordeal, which "must ever, to my mind, rank amongst the most noble, the most sublime pieces of history of the century in which we are living," demonstrating triumphantly "the metal of which English-speaking men are made." At Christmas it was especially appropriate to show the survivors of this ordeal "that we honour, as it deserves, the work they have done for the world since the election of 1860, and can sympathize with their high hopes for the future of their continent with no jealousy or distrust, as brethren of the same stock, and children of the same Father."[10]

On the American side, there was lingering resentment of British neutrality, which had at times seemed suspiciously pro-Southern, during the conflict. Hughes's attempts to persuade the North that neutrality did not signify indifference and that the noisy English voices attacking the Union and defending the Confederacy had not spoken for the nation began as early as 1864, before the war had ended.

In that year, Hughes was asked to donate a manuscript to a fair held in New York to raise funds for the Union cause. Not only did he comply, but he also wrote an eloquent letter to the editor of the newspaper published by the fair in which, after expressing his own sympathy with the North, he argued that, with the one prominent exception of his old hero Carlyle (he might have mentioned his old friend Kingsley as well), "'almost the whole weight of English thought has been on the side of freedom.'" Largely because of the influence wielded by anonymous journalists, Hughes concedes, "'the lion's share'" of the blame for the "'estrangement and bitterness which have arisen between our countries since the war broke out'" is England's; but he does complain, in the most tactful way conceivable, "'that even the best and fairest men amongst you have never yet done justice, either to the conduct of our Government, beset as they

have been with questions of no common difficulty on all sides, or
to the attitude of the thinking portion of our community.' " In closing,
Hughes expresses his hope for " 'a closer and more hearty alliance
between my country and yours, as soon as this war is over, than has
been possible since we parted in last century.' "[11] When peace finally
came, Hughes worked tirelessly for such an alliance.

His first trip to the United States, from late August to October
1870, gave Hughes a golden opportunity to pursue this work. Feted
and lionized by his hosts wherever he went, he spent "the greater
part of my time in showing them how mistaken they must be in
their views as to England, else how is it that we didn't interfere
and get to war."[12] In his private conversations with Americans,
Hughes wanted to "help to heal wounded pride and other sorely
irritating places in the over-sensitive, but simple and gallant Yankee
mind";[13] and, though he fended off "numerous and urgent" requests
that he deliver public lectures in which he might expound his views
to even more people, he finally came to believe "that I ought not to
leave the country without giving one at any rate, and all my friends
said that the Music Hall in Boston was the place if I only spoke
once."[14]

Hughes addressed a distinguished and appreciative Boston audience
on October 11.[15] His calling the speech "John to Jonathan" was an
obvious reference to Lowell's "Jonathan to John" (1862), a statement of the Northern case directed to John Bull in the wake of the
Trent affair; and the whole lecture may be taken as a belated response
to that poem, particularly to the reproach voiced in ll. 91–94:

> We know we've got a cause, John,
>   Thet's honest, just, an' true;
> We thought 't would win applause, John,
>   Ef nowheres else, from you.

It was Hughes's thesis that the Union "cause" did "win applause"
in England, far more than Lowell and his compatriots realized at the
time. Though there were swings in public opinion during the war,
the great majority of Englishmen "were the staunch friends of the
North from the very outset" ("John," 84). As for the English government, its actions were not anti-Northern: the queen's proclamation
of neutrality a month after the firing on Fort Sumter may have
been premature and somewhat tactless, but it had been urged on her

by friends of the North who "wanted to stop letters of marque and to legitimize the captures made by your blockading squadron" ("John," 88). Certainly neutrality was preferable to the only feasible alternative, recognition of the Confederate States, and that the government would not accept. Now, the war having ended, England was prepared to submit the troublesome *Alabama* claims to arbitration; in any case, he reminded his audience, "the *Alabama* was the only one of the rebel cruisers of whose character our Government had any notice, which escaped from our harbours" ("John," 89).

Hughes concluded the Boston address with his answer to a question raised by his "very dear and old friend" Lowell in "Jonathan to John" (ll. 109–10):

> Shall it be love, or hate, John?
> It's you thet's to decide....

England has decided, Hughes asserted. "It will be love and not hate between the two freeest of the great nations of the earth, if our decision can so settle it." Apparently alluding to the general election of July 1865, three months after Appomattox, which made Members of Parliament of Hughes and John Stuart Mill and otherwise strengthened the radical wing of the Liberal party, Hughes said: "In England the dam that had for so many years held back the free waters burst in the same year that you sheathed your sword, and now your friends there are triumphant and honoured; and if those who were your foes ever return to power you will find that the lesson of your war has not been lost on them." He foresaw a time, not far distant, when these two "great nations," sharing the same heritage as well as the same language, would work together in amity to establish "free and happy communities" around the earth "in which the angels' message of peace and good-will amongst men may not be still a mockery and delusion" ("John," 91).

Before a decade had passed, Hughes himself was to play a major role in founding what he hoped would be one such community.

Rugby, Tennessee. The complicated and bittersweet story of the rise and fall of the Rugby settlement in northeastern Tennessee and of Hughes's part in it has been told in considerable detail elsewhere.[16] Here we must concentrate on the one text into which Hughes poured all of his high hopes for the colony, a rather short book with a very long title: *Rugby, Tennessee: Being Some Account of the Settlement Founded on the Cumberland Plateau by the Board of Aid to Land Ownership, Limited, a Company Incorporated in England, and Authorised to Hold and Deal in Land by Act of the Legislature of the State of Tennessee, with a Report on the Soils of the Plateau by the Hon. F. W. Killebrew, A.M. Ph.D., Commissioner of Agriculture for the State.* Like *The Old Church* of three years earlier, *Rugby, Tennessee* (1881) was something of a pastiche, consisting largely of essays already published and speeches already delivered. It probably owed its appearance in volume form chiefly to Hughes's desire to raise funds for this American venture, his longtime publisher Macmillan having agreed to give Hughes "all the profits but a 'modest percentage to pay costs out of pocket,' in order that he might use the money for 'needed public buildings and improvements at Rugby.' "[17]

Our consideration of *Rugby, Tennessee* is enriched if we recall that Hughes had long entertained the notion that young Englishmen who had reached a dead end at home should think about going abroad to make a fresh start in life. Twenty years before this book was published, in chapter 35 of *Tom Brown at Oxford*, Tom and Hardy discussed "the advantages of emigration," which here seemed to mean getting away from old England in the company of "graceful women" and "beautiful children" and literally carving out a new and idyllic existence in some far-off primeval wilderness. Though the obviously amused narrator dismissed this utopian talk by a couple of undergraduates as "castle-building," the passage does contain an uncanny foreshadowing of Hughes's later vision of the Tennessee Rugby, especially in these two sentences: "The log-houses would also contain fascinating select libraries, continually reinforced from home, sufficient to keep all dwellers in the happy clearing in communion with all the highest minds of their own and former generations. Wondrous games in the neighbouring forest, dear old home customs established and taking root in the wilderness, with ultimate dainty flower gardens, conservatories, and pianofortes—a millennium on a small scale, with universal education, competence, prosperity, and equal rights!" (*Oxford*, 387).

About ten years later, during the same American journey on which he delivered his "John to Jonathan" speech, Hughes again reflected on the subject of emigration, this time viewing it somewhat less fancifully than he had done in *Tom Brown at Oxford*. After returning home, he contributed to *Macmillan's Magazine* a series of obviously autobiographical sketches describing an Englishman's trip by train from Niagara Falls to Sioux City along the same route that Hughes himself had followed. In the first of these pieces, the narrator asks one of his traveling companions—another Englishman, who here sounds very much like Hughes—if the fact that he has been poring over some brochures designed to lure foreign settlers to various western states means that he himself might emigrate.

"No, no; my roots are too deep in the old soil. The fact is, I have several long-legged, strapping boys growing up, and, like most of the youngsters in the Old World, they won't take kindly to the beaten ways of life. Somehow, our atmosphere is electric, and the whole of society is slipping away from its moorings. Latin and Greek for ten or twelve years, and the three learned professions to follow, won't hold English boys. They will swarm off, and I, for one, can't say they're wrong. So the point is, to find where they can light with the best chances."[18]

These passages—one from the early 1860s and the other from the early 1870s—anticipate two of the major themes of *Rugby, Tennessee*. One is idealistic: life under the right conditions in the new world can satisfy the frustrated aspirations of ardent youths like Tom Brown. The other is more practical: emigration, again under the right conditions, will drain off from England an ominously growing surplus of highly educated but underutilized men. *Rugby, Tennessee* also enunciates a third important theme, which might be called political, and which builds on Hughes's earlier emphasis on the need to forge secure links between Britain and the United States: for the sake of closer understanding and friendship between the two countries, England should send "all that can be spared of our best blood into the United States."[19]

Of the three parts into which *Rugby, Tennessee* is divided, only the first consists of new material by Hughes. Appropriately for someone who contributed from time to time to the *Spectator*, Hughes named this section "Our Will Wimbles," after a character in the early eighteenth-century periodical essays by the same title. Joseph Addison's original Will Wimble, descended from an ancient family, was an accomplished, amiable, and popular man who had nothing worthwhile to occupy his time. He was "wholly employed in trifles," typical in that respect "of many a younger brother of a great family, who had rather see their children starve like gentlemen, than thrive in a trade or profession."[20]

In the final quarter of the nineteenth century, Hughes points out, England is full of Will Wimbles. There has been a "vast increase of public schools in England" and also a resurgence "of the old grammar schools . . . into new life." Such establishments are attracting not only the offspring of the aristocracy and the squirearchy, but also "sons of professional men, manufacturers, merchants," and "the aims and methods of the education they are giving have improved as rapidly as the numbers requiring it have increased" (*Rugby*, 4). In Hughes's judgment, these schools have succeeded admirably not only in imparting classical learning but also in building character.

What is to be done with all the well-educated and well-trained young men they have produced? There is not room for them in "the three learned professions, the public service, and the press. Art and science . . . offer at present too few and too special careers" (*Rugby*, 5). Of those who come from the aristocracy or the landed gentry, the great majority cannot, as younger sons, hope to succeed to their fathers' titles or estates. That leaves only three other obvious possibilities, each unattractive for one reason or another: trade, manual labor, or idleness.

Whatever the virtues of commerce may be in the abstract, in practical terms it is not an appealing option for these young men. In an age when, in Hughes's not unbiased view, Carlyle's denunciations of the "Gospel of Mammonism" have been widely influential and the idea that cooperation should replace competition in business and manufacturing is gaining more and more adherents, "it is plain that the spirit of our highest culture and the spirit of our trade do not agree together" (*Rugby*, 5). At school the modern Will Wimble, even if he is himself the son of a businessman, has been taught to honor "scrupulousness—a scorn of anything like sharpness or meanness—in money matters . . . and so he is as rapidly becoming as averse to, and as unfitted for, the practices of ordinary competitive trade as the son of a squire or parson" (*Rugby*, 12). Besides, there are not as many opportunities in trade as there were in earlier, economically more buoyant, times. W. H. G. Armytage explains Hughes's glancing reference to "these last few years of deep depression" (*Rugby*, 6) by remarking that "the rise of Germany, the consequent slump of 1878–79 in England, and the shrinkage of the British share in the world

markets lessened the number of outlets for the public schoolmen produced in ever-increasing numbers on the Tom Brown pattern."[21]

As to manual labor, which Hughes—following Emerson, from
whose "Man the Reformer" he quotes at length—praises warmly,
that is not for the Will Wimbles either, at any rate in the England
of the present day. Still voicing some of his Christian Socialist convictions, Hughes does predict that the future belongs to those whom
he calls "our handicraftsmen," and he concedes that "it seems not
improbable that the Will Wimbles in another generation may find
their best chance of satisfactory daily bread, and general usefulness,
in some form of manual labour at home." Until that time arrives,
however, "the handicraftsman's career is not really open to anyone
not born in the ranks," because of "the jealousy and distrust of the
working class, and the prejudice of their own against what would
be considered loss of caste" (*Rugby*, 20).

As unacceptable as trade or manual labor, though for different
reasons, is enforced idleness. Hughes is saddened and appalled by the
growing number of "fine strong fellows" with no appropriate work
to do: "hopeful still, ready to do *anything*, so that they may only be
independent and a burthen to nobody," instead "of first-rate human
material going helplessly to waste, and in too many cases beginning
to turn sour, and taint, instead of strengthening, the national life"
(*Rugby*, 6).

Having outlined the problem in the first three chapters of part I
of *Rugby, Tennessee*, Hughes proceeds in the fourth to explain the
solution he has in mind. The only course open to the Will Wimbles
of Victorian England is to follow Emerson's advice and "begin the
world anew, as he does who puts the spade into the ground for
food."[22] Because "the present caste prejudice against manual labour
is too strong" to allow them to take spade in hand at home, and
because "land here is too costly a luxury" to allow them to work
English ground, they "must begin, then, across the seas somewhere—
the sooner the better" (*Rugby*, 25). This means emigration, preferably
to a carefully chosen setting where they can live by the values they
have learned: "a place where what we have been calling the English
public-school spirit—the spirit of hardiness, of reticence, of scrupulousness in all money matters, of cordial fellowship, shall be recognised
and prevail" (*Rugby*, 25–26).

As its name is meant to suggest, the Rugby settlement in Tennessee is just such a place, where an educated young Englishman will

find ready access to rewarding and respected labor and to inexpensive housing and land. He will live there amid conditions that Hughes—ever the advocate of the cooperative movement and the national church—is convinced will redound to his moral and spiritual welfare, buying what he needs at a community-owned commissary devoid of "the old tricks and frauds of trade" characteristic of shops run for profit, and attending "one church which is open to all, and which invites to a common worship, being the property of no single denomination, but of the community" (*Rugby*, 27). This community will mold the individual by bringing out the best that is in him, just as he by his exertions will help to build a stronger community.

If the above summary of part I makes Hughes's vision of the Rugby scheme sound more austere than it really is, there is no such problem in part II, "A New Home—First Impressions." This consists of reprints of eight predominantly lighthearted essays that Hughes sent to the *Spectator* in the late summer and autumn of 1880 from Tennessee, where he had gone for the official opening of the colony in his capacity as president of the Board of Aid to Land Ownership. Here, he stresses the conviviality of the community, the beauty of its setting, and the attractive qualities of the natives, and expresses optimism that his dream of a "public-school paradise" in the mountains of Tennessee will come true.

That life in this remote Rugby can be jolly is impressed on Hughes as soon as he arrives there. He is met at the little railway station some seven miles from the town site by a small band of cheerful Englishmen, unmistakably public-school products despite the frontier garb they wear, and they make a merry party of their rough ride to the settlement. This is still only a "city of the future" (*Rugby*, 41), but the food he is served there is plentiful and the company is excellent. Hughes is astonished to find a beautifully groomed tennis court ready for play in the midst of unfinished houses and public buildings—one symbol of the settlers' determination to carry with them to Tennessee as many of the amenities of English life as they could.

The rugged, isolated Cumberland Plateau is no White Horse Vale, but this only adds to its charms for Hughes. He is enchanted by "the new flora and fauna" (*Rugby*, 56) he encounters in the woods, and he finds that "you can't live many days up here without getting to love the trees even more, I think, than we do in well-kempt England" (*Rugby*, 54). Having recently left "the great heat of New York,

Newport, and Cincinnati," he rejoices at "the freshness and delight of this brisk mountain air" (*Rugby*, 36).

Hughes's attitude toward the mountaineers of northeastern Tennessee is oddly ambivalent. He concedes that they are shiftless and too fond of illegally distilled "moonshine" whiskey for their own good, and he calls their women "dreadful slatterns" (*Rugby*, 65); but he considers it "a pleasure" to get to know them, and indignantly rejects the frequent references to them as " 'mean whites,' 'poor white trash' and the like, in novels, travels, and newspapers" (*Rugby*, 61). What, then, are their redeeming features? For one thing, they were staunchly pro-Union during the Civil War. Moreover, though mostly very poor, they are hospitable and honest, and their wit—their adeptness at "quaint and ready replies" (*Rugby*, 66)—is appealing. A late-twentieth-century reader is likely to wince at Hughes's blithe depictions of the blacks in the area as grinning darkies, but he does point out that in his experience they are marginally less lazy than the local whites and much less willing to sell their votes. There is nothing backhanded in Hughes's praise of the blacks' determination to get their children educated.

Hughes's faith in the future of this colony is perhaps best expressed in part II of *Rugby, Tennessee* in the final chapter, "The Opening Day," an account of the festivities associated with the dedication of the settlement on October 5, 1880. Presided over by the Episcopal Bishop of Tennessee, the ceremony is a most impressive one, despite a number of mishaps. When it is over and the distinguished visitors have left, those who remain behind are imbued with "a sense of strength gained for the work of building up a community which shall know how to comport itself in good and bad times, and shall help, instead of hindering, its sons and daughters in leading a brave, simple, and Christian life" (*Rugby*, 91).

As it turned out, of course, the Rugby settlement was unable to survive "bad times," but it would not be quite fair to use our hindsight to condemn Hughes for the buoyant optimism of part II or accuse him of engaging in the sort of "castle-building" for which he had teased Tom Brown and Hardy twenty years earlier. It is true that Hughes was always rather too prone to indulge in wishful thinking about his visionary schemes. To do him justice, however, we must recall that he was aware of this trait in himself. In the third chapter, for example, he raises a troubling question and immediately answers it in characteristic fashion, with ruefully qualified self-confidence. "The thought occurs, are our swans—our visions, already so bright, of splendid crops, and simple life, to be raised and lived in this fairy-land—to prove geese? I hope not. It would be the downfall of the last castle in Spain I am ever likely to build" (*Rugby*, 46).

In the final part of *Rugby, Tennessee* the tone shifts again. It consists of four chapters, alternately inspirational and practical in nature, but each making essentially the same main point: there is every reason to suppose that, if everyone does his part, this settlement can be, not a "castle in Spain," but a new Jerusalem.

Hughes begins with the text of the address he gave, as president of the Board of Aid, on the opening day of the Tennessee Rugby. Its mission, he says, is an exalted one. Uniting as it does the labors of English settlers on American soil with the financial and moral backing of men on both sides of the Atlantic, it is an outgrowth of the deep conviction "that the future of our own race; and indeed of the world, in which our race is so clearly destined to play the leading part; can never be what it should be, until the most cordial alliance, the most intimate relations, have been established firmly, without any risk or possibility of disturbance or misunderstanding between its two great branches" (*Rugby*, 93). In this "swarming time of the race," "a time of great movement of population" (*Rugby*, 95), it is especially important that this mission be carried out in accordance with carefully defined principles, and these Hughes proceeds to list.

To proclaim that Rugby will be a community is not very helpful. Such a statement may suggest, misleadingly, that it will embody the features of the kind of centralized communism advocated in Europe by Marx and Lassalle "and on this continent by very inferior, and even more violent and anarchic, persons." Nothing could be further from the truth. Throughout his involvement with the Christian Socialist, cooperative, and trade-union movements, Hughes advocated a very minimal role for government in economic life, and so he is being perfectly consistent in disavowing state socialism here, as well as in his subsequent rejection of "a paternal state, the owner of all property, finding easy employment and liberal maintenance for all citizens, reserving all profits for the community, and paying no dividends to individuals." Nor does he want anyone to associate Rugby with earlier utopian "communistic experiments here or in Europe" (*Rugby*, 96), experiments that have regularly failed.

The members of a community must have something in common, and it is necessary to explain what that something—that common spirit behind Rugby—is. In Hughes's view, it means taking "this lovely corner of God's earth which has been entrusted to us," treating "it lovingly and reverently," and using it for "the common good" (*Rugby*, 96–97). By the latter phrase, as any reader of this study will readily infer, Hughes means far more than material well-being. The development and use of land and the design and construction of buildings must be such as to educate "the eye and mind" (*Rugby*, 98). In order to get "rid once for all of the evils which have turned retail trade into a keen and anxious and, generally, a dishonest scramble in older communities" (*Rugby*, 101), business must be conducted along cooperative lines, not only in the commissary but also in the thriving cattle industry that Hughes envisages. The essential religious life of the community, too, must foster harmony and fellowship among the residents: though there will be one church, holding Anglican services, members of other denominations will be welcome to use the building "as a pledge of Christian brotherhood and an acknowledgment that, however far apart our courses may seem to lie, we steer by one compass and seek one port" (*Rugby*, 104). In short, "our aim and hope are to plant on these highlands a community of gentlemen and ladies"—not "the joint product of feudalism and wealth" one finds in a traditional aristocratic society, but rather dedicated men and women who are proud to live "by the labour of their own hands" (*Rugby*, 106) in pursuit of their common goals.

By contrast with this lofty statement, the second chapter of part III concerns itself with some very down-to-earth matters. Reprinted from an article, also called "Rugby, Tennessee," in the February 1881 number of *Macmillan's Magazine*, it answers such practical questions as who should consider going to the colony, what he should take, how he can get there from England most cheaply and expeditiously, and what he can expect to find once he arrives.

But it too contains an idealistic strain. Life in Rugby will be hard, Hughes warns, but when the settler's daily work is done he will find much to occupy his mind and spirit. In a probably unconscious echo of the reference to "fascinating select libraries" in the passage from *Tom Brown at Oxford* quoted earlier in this chapter, Hughes points with special pride to the "good library" already in existence in the infant settlement. He again adverts to the contribution Rugby will make to Anglo-American friendship, adding that its location in the

American South will contribute to another political goal for which all Englishmen should work. "What we English want, looking to the future, is, not only that England and America should be fast friends, but that the feeling of union in the States themselves should be developed as soundly and rapidly as possible—that all wounds should be healed, and all breaches closed, finally and for ever—for the sake of our race and of mankind. Much still remains to be done for this end, and I am convinced that a good stream of Englishmen into the Southern States may and will materially help on the good cause" (*Rugby*, 118).

Part III of *Rugby, Tennessee* also contains the text of another speech by Hughes, this one delivered at the English Rugby School on April 7, 1881. This third chapter combines the inspirational tone of the first (explaining the ethos behind the Tennessee settlement) and the practical tone of the second (explaining what life there is like), and bases its argument on the thesis of part I: that emigrating to a place like the new Rugby is the best thing a young Englishman can do if he is unable to find any appropriate outlet for his talents and his training at home after leaving an institution like the old Rugby. The fact that Hughes, now nearly sixty years of age, has returned there to address an audience of schoolboys accounts for a certain playful cast to his remarks, especially near the beginning; but it also lends a certain solemnity to his message. Abandoning for the moment his several roles as a prominent public figure, Hughes makes it clear that he is staking his reputation as an Old Rugbeian on the integrity of the vision he depicts.

Especially right after this moving speech, chapter 4 of part III may seem something of an anticlimax. Entitled "Colonel Killebrew's Report," it is a detailed account by the Tennessee commissioner of agriculture—who is, in a sense, also staking his reputation on what he is saying—of what he believes to be the economic potential of the region chosen for the Rugby colony. Marguerite B. Hamer's characterization of this report as "none too flattering" tells only part of the story.[23] What Killebrew says, in prose that is remarkably measured and matter-of-fact, is that, though the soil of the Cumberland Plateau is "comparatively thin and infertile," "it is far superior to any soils found in New England outside the valleys" (*Rugby*, 138); with proper cultivation and due attention to which crops will flourish there, it can be made highly productive. Moreover, because of its rail connections with Cincinnati, Atlanta, and the larger towns of

Tennessee, Rugby and its environs could serve those markets with advantage. Given the abundance of timber and mineral deposits around the settlement, it might well turn into a manufacturing as well as an agricultural center. Implicit in Killebrew's statement, however, there is one very important proviso: "patient labour, guided by skill and intelligence" (*Rugby*, 159), must be lavished on this rugged virgin area if its potential is to be realized. His report indicates very clearly what "great errors and mistakes" (*Rugby*, 158) must be avoided if Rugby is to prosper.

That it ultimately failed does not detract from the soundness of Killebrew's advice—or, for that matter, from the nobility of Hughes's dreams for it.

Chapter Five

The Biographies

In 1869, Thomas Hughes published *Alfred the Great*, the first of six biographies that were to occupy much of his spare time during the next twenty years. *Memoir of a Brother*—George Hughes, who was born at Uffington thirteen months before him—appeared in 1873. Nine years later there followed the *Memoir of Daniel Macmillan*, cofounder of the publishing firm named after him and his brother Alexander. In the *Life and Times of Peter Cooper* (1886), Hughes gave an account of the American entrepreneur and philanthropist who is best remembered today as the founder of the Cooper Union in New York City. *James Fraser* (1887) was the biography of a churchman who achieved distinction as Bishop of Manchester. And the last of the series, *David Livingstone* (1889), chronicled the career of the medical missionary who became a national celebrity by virtue of his African explorations.

Though at first glance the subjects of these biographies appear to have little in common, there are in fact some significant links among them. In their different spheres, all six men—even the intensely private and, until the appearance of the *Memoir of a Brother*, virtually unknown George Hughes—played heroic roles, contending with adversity of every imaginable kind. Except for King Alfred, they all had their blemishes, but each lived a life worthy in some important way of admiration and emulation. Except for Peter Cooper, whose religion was something of an enigma for Hughes, they were all devout Christians; and even Cooper's motives and achievements could be construed in Christian terms by a writer who always insisted that human endeavors must be consistent with the will of God.

Hughes felt a large measure of affinity with each of his subjects. This was even true of Alfred, who had lived a thousand years before him; for, like Hughes, he was a son of Berkshire, born at Wantage, just south of the Vale of the White Horse, and Hughes could never forget this. The Wessex king's associations with Hughes's own county, especially his military exploits there, had already been mentioned in glowing terms in *Tom Brown's School Days* and featured prominently in *The Scouring of the White Horse,* and Hughes's enthusiasm for Alfred was so keen that he had no hesitation about elevating him to the status of a Carlylean hero.[1]

Hughes's other five subjects, his contemporaries, were drawn on a more human scale. Apparently he never met David Livingstone, and this may account for the relative remoteness of his treatment of that remarkable figure in the history of imperialism; but Hughes could certainly sympathize with Livingstone's ardent Christianity and identify with his burning hatred of Negro slavery. The other four, however, played important roles in Hughes's own life, and with the first three he was on intimate terms.

When Thomas Hughes was a boy and a young man, George Hughes was everything to him that an older brother should be to a younger. Until George went up to Oxford in January 1841, when Tom was eighteen, they were rarely apart; they later lived with or near each other in Oxford and in London. James Fraser, long before his rise in the church, had been Hughes's tutor at Oriel College, and the two remained friends until Fraser's death. Hughes had known Daniel Macmillan for about a decade before he died in June 1857, just two months after *Tom Brown's School Days* had come out with the Macmillan imprint. Theirs was much more of a personal than an author-publisher relationship: drawn together by their affectionate loyalty to Maurice, both had participated in the Christian Socialist movement, and Hughes had served as godfather to one of Macmillan's sons.[2] By the time Hughes made his first American tour, Peter Cooper had become a semiofficial greeter of foreign dignitaries visiting New York City. Hughes stayed in Cooper's house in September 1870 and was charmed by his host, calling him in a letter home "one of the most guileless and sweetest of old men."[3] As a founder and veteran staff member of the Working Men's College, Hughes was most favorably impressed by the Cooper Union, which he regarded as a remarkably successful counterpart of the London institution.

Hughes, then, clearly had the kind of sympathy with his subjects that is normally a prerequisite to success in writing biography. And yet none of these books can fairly be called a memorable example of that genre. Why is this so? Each of Hughes's biographies presents its own difficulties, of course, and we shall examine some of these in this chapter; but there is one problem that is common to them all: they were written as acts of duty or piety rather than as labors of love by an author who did not always find the work either easy or congenial.

Three of these biographies were commissioned by Hughes's old friend and admirer Alexander Macmillan: *Alfred the Great* to continue his firm's "Sunday Library" of books with a significant religious dimension,[4] the *Memoir of Daniel Macmillan* to pay tribute to his late brother, and *David Livingstone* to launch an "English Men of Action" series, comparable to the successful "English Men of Letters," also published by Macmillan. Surviving members of their families persuaded Hughes to undertake the biographies of Cooper and Fraser; and he himself conceived the idea of writing George Hughes's life for the sake of the instruction he hoped it would afford to the sons of both brothers.

Having made up his mind to carry out these tasks, Hughes found himself overwhelmed with material. Over forty years' immersion in the West Country legends about King Alfred could not by themselves result in a respectable book: as Hughes was aware, there was also the work of countless historians, philologists, and chroniclers, going all the way back to Alfred's own lifetime, to come to terms with, not to mention the large body of writings attributed to Alfred himself. As to Hughes's nineteenth-century subjects, they had all been indefatigable correspondents and diarists, and each left behind him masses of paper to confound his would-be biographer. Livingstone was especially problematical for Hughes: he had had no personal knowledge of the man, and he could bring to the materials he consulted only a general sense of Livingstone's significance and a layman's sketchy acquaintance with the geography and history of the continent where he did his work. Even when Hughes was intimately familiar with his subjects, however, he tended to let his evidence speak for itself, failing to subordinate it adequately to a thesis or a narrative line of his own. The result, all too often, is that the reader is nearly as intimidated by the results of Hughes's labors as Hughes must have been when he began them.

There is a related problem that is common to all six of Hughes's biographies. Though he leaves the reader with a distinct sense of the accomplishments of each man whose story he tells, he backs away from anything more than a superficial examination of his inner life.

For example, while scrupulously providing evidence that Daniel Macmillan and David Livingstone endured spells of spiritual torment, Hughes is equally scrupulous about refraining from any searching attempt to account for such anguish or to connect it with his subjects' more characteristic religious affirmations. Like most Victorian biographers, Hughes averts his eyes from areas of private experience that modern readers expect to have treated with some candor, and this too has doubtless impaired the durability of these books.

Alfred the Great

The earliest of Hughes's biographies stands apart from its successors in several important respects. Much of its distinctiveness grows out of the obvious fact that, alone among Hughes's protagonists, Alfred was a great and famous king—a king, moreover, who had reigned so long before Hughes wrote that much of his life was either shrouded in obscurity or else encrusted with legend. Nevertheless, Hughes did his best to establish the facts of that life, making such use as he could of the sources that were available to him.[5]

It is clear, however, that Hughes was not nearly as interested in factual precision, which was not attainable in this case anyway, as he was in drawing out the lessons that Alfred's life and works could teach a mid-Victorian audience. *Alfred the Great* is first and foremost a tract for the times, designed to instruct Hughes's contemporaries in the true nature and purpose of government. All too often beguiled by the shibboleths of parliamentary reform or the rhetoric of popular revolution, they needed to learn what could be accomplished—what, a thousand years earlier, had been accomplished—by an authentic Christian king striving to do God's will and establish God's law in his realm.

The presence of Thomas Carlyle looms larger in *Alfred the Great* than it does in any of Hughes's other writings. For more than thirty years, that Scottish sage had been articulating a cruel dilemma to the large audiences who attended his lectures and read his essays and books: on the one hand, modern rulers, however potent they fancied themselves to be, were incapable of solving the problems that afflicted their societies; but, on the other hand, there was every reason to believe that democratic government could do no better, and would probably do much worse.

By 1869, when Hughes wrote his preface to *Alfred the Great*, that dilemma had reached an acute stage. In his own country, the time-honored constitutional role of the House of Lords had been called into serious question by its foot-dragging on a major piece of legislation, the Irish Church Bill. Across the English Channel in France, the Second Empire of Louis Napoleon was coming apart at the seams. Indeed, everywhere in the civilized world the "practical need of examining once more the principles upon which society, and the life of nations, rest" was becoming urgent. As Hughes phrased the question, "How are nations to be saved from the tyranny or domination of arbitrary will, whether of a Caesar or a mob?"[6] The answer, he suggested, had been provided long ago by Carlyle, "the teacher, prophet, seer—call him what you will—who has in many ways moved more deeply than any other the hearts of this generation" (*Alfred*, 7), and he announces the line he himself will take by beginning his first chapter with the opening two sentences of Carlyle's "The Hero as King."[7]

Carlyle argued that only the kind of leader whom he called "the God-made king" (*Alfred*, 7)[8]—a wise, just, and devout hero who perceives the will of God and is able to make it prevail—could resolve the dilemma by reconciling the need for strong governance with the demands of the masses and so rescuing his people from stagnation, strife, and despair. In preaching this message, Hughes says, Carlyle was adapting the teachings of the Bible to the Victorian age, for his view of the hero-king in touch with the divine as the champion and savior of the nation "fills at least as large a space in our sacred books as in Mr. Carlyle's" (*Alfred,* 12).

One of the most striking facts about the hero as Carlyle defines him is that, by virtue of the special qualities that confer this status on him, he is able to bring order out of chaos. Hughes's Alfred clearly meets Carlyle's test.

For one thing, he took over a war-ravaged kingdom and—thanks to his courage, his military prowess, his resilience in defeat, and his magnanimity in victory—managed to bring it to a state as close to peace as was conceivable in the turbulent Europe of his day. In the middle of the ninth century, when Alfred was an infant, the Viking Danes had gained a foothold in southeastern England. Their incursions increased in number, intensity, and duration, and they achieved control over more and more of the island until by the winter of 870–71 they menaced Alfred's nation of Wessex, then ruled by his brother Ethel-red. Alfred's first great victory over the Danes occurred in 871 at the battle of Ashdown, celebrated by Hughes in *The Scouring of the White Horse;* later that year Ethelred died and Alfred succeeded to his brother's crown. Under Alfred's direction, the struggle against the invaders went on until their defeat at Ethandene (modern Edington) in Wiltshire in 878.

But Alfred's troubles with the Danes were by no means over. They were left in control of a considerable portion of England, and Danish raids on Alfred's kingdom continued, those led by a marauding chieftain named Haesten, or Hasting, being especially damaging. Nevertheless, a large measure of tranquility was restored to Wessex during the last two decades of Alfred's brief life,[9] and he took this opportunity to introduce a number of far-reaching reforms into his realm.

In Hughes's account, ninth-century Wessex was badly in need of reforming. During the reign of Alfred's grandfather Egbert between 802 and 839, the people prospered, but corruption grew as they became more selfish and materialistic. Under Ethelwulf, Egbert's son and Alfred's father, morality deteriorated even more: "the inner and spiritual life of the nation was consequently dying out, and the people were falling into a dull, mechanical habit of mind. Their religion had become chiefly a matter of custom and routine; and, as a sure consequence, a sensual and grovelling life was spreading through all classes" (*Alfred,* 130–31).

By mid-century, the West Saxons had sunk so low that some kind of divine visitation was inevitable. This, Hughes insists in a passage blending past and present that Carlyle himself might have written, is how God intervenes in human history, in the nineteenth century as much as the ninth. When a nation places private gain above public virtue, "men who love their country will welcome Danish invasions, civil wars, potato diseases, cotton famines, Fenian agitations, whatever calamity may be needed to awake the higher life again, and bid the nation arise and live" (*Alfred,* 131).

Just as Alfred's Christian faith enabled him to survive adversity and lead his people to victory over the pagan Danes, so it endowed him with the wisdom and the skill to govern justly and to rebuild his nation, both physically and spiritually, once there was respite from conflict. When he framed his legal code, for example, Alfred was careful to make it conform to the moral teachings of the Bible, remembering what modern lawgivers too often forget: that secular law, if it is to be effective and enduring, must be based on divine law. In the administration of justice, Alfred was determined to draw clear lines of accountability and mutual responsibility in a manner that should be instructive in Hughes's own day, when the doctrine of "every man for himself" laid down by laissez-faire economists has become rampant, making "English life more and more disjointed." "What we specially want is something which shall bind us more closely together. . . . The need of getting done in some form that which frank-pledge did for Alfred's people expresses itself . . . in our co-operative movement, and trades unions" (*Alfred*, 186–87).

Regardless of how forms of government may change, Hughes argues, it is as true in 1869 as it was a thousand years earlier that the real ruler of the nation is God and that any temporal ruler must obey and enforce God's law if he is to be successful and govern a genuinely prosperous people. King Alfred's career is eloquent testimony to this eternal truth and embodies a great lesson for the modern statesman. "Kings, priests, judges, whatever men succeed to, or usurp, or are thrust into power, come immediately under that eternal government which the God of the nation has established, and the order of which cannot be violated with impunity. Every ruler who ignores or defies it saps the national life and prosperity, and brings trouble on his country, sometimes swiftly, but always surely" (*Alfred*, 322).

That lesson will lose none of its validity when the institution of monarchy fades into history, as it surely will very soon. "All the signs of our time tell us that the day of earthly kings has gone by, and the advent to power of the great body of the people, those who live by manual labour, is at hand. . . . In England, the co-operative movement, and the organization of the trade societies, should be enough to prove this, to any one who has eyes, and is open to conviction" (*Alfred*, 332). But our new rulers, no less than the old, Hughes maintains, will have to conform to God's laws, or they too will be swept away.

The fact that *Alfred the Great* appeared in Macmillan's "Sunday Library" series obliged Hughes to adopt "a religious point of view" and to address himself to "a Christian public" in writing the book (*Alfred*, 317). But this involved no strain on his part. He was writing from conviction—as a Christian, as an admirer of King Alfred, as a disciple of Carlyle, as an early leader of the cooperative movement, and as an author who believed in the propriety of preaching his convictions no matter what his ostensible subject might be.

This didactic note is at least as prominent in *Alfred the Great* as in the other works by Hughes we have examined so far, resounding most insistently in the first chapter ("Of Kings and Kingship") and the last ("The End of the Whole Matter"). It is also to be heard in chapter 11 ("Retrospect"), where Hughes pauses to reflect on the meaning of Alfred's victory over the Danish invaders and provides a transition between the two main sections of the book. But it is clear throughout *Alfred the Great* that Hughes's chief purpose is to teach. The first part, consisting of chapters 2 through 10, is largely narrative, telling the story of Alfred's life through the years of the war against the Danes; the second section, chapters 12 through 25, is predominantly expository, discussing Alfred's works of peace. Every chapter except one begins with a biblical epigraph, which is then illustrated in what follows. For instance, the scriptural text at the head of chapter 4—"Wherewithal shall a young man cleanse his way? / Even by ruling himself after thy word" (Psalms 119:9)— precedes Hughes's account of a youthful Alfred fighting down carnal desire by means of prayer.

Though it has been superseded by more recent scholarship, *Alfred the Great* can still be read with pleasure and profit. The most artfully constructed of Hughes's six biographies, it conveys a clear and unified impression of what Alfred meant to Hughes and why he believed this subject was of such great importance to his contemporaries.

Memoir of a Brother

The protagonist of Hughes's next biography represents a striking contrast to King Alfred. Whereas Alfred had been widely renowned for centuries, George Hughes was hardly known outside his family circle. A barrister like his younger brother, he did not use the law as a springboard to public life; indeed, he only practiced briefly before becoming a country gentleman and devoting himself, not quite happily, to private pursuits. George Hughes died, as obscurely as he had lived, on May 2, 1872, in his fifty-first year. Matthew Arnold wrote Thomas Hughes a kind letter of condolence three weeks later; like the other old friends whose expressions of sympathy are recorded in the *Memoir of a Brother*, Arnold had known George as a boy and young man and referred nostalgically to those early days without saying much about George's recent accomplishments. In truth, there had not been any of which such correspondents would have been aware.

How can the biography of such a recluse be justified? As he says in the preface, Hughes originally wrote the *Memoir* "for, and at the request of," George's "near relatives, and intimate friends."[10] Dedicating it to his nephews and sons, he stresses the need for the next generation to know something of "the head of the family of which you are members" (*Memoir*, xi). His account of George Hughes's life, he tells them, should "help to turn you more trustfully and lovingly" to emulating Christ, "that source of all truth, all strength, all light" (*Memoir*, xiii), whose example George himself unfailingly followed.

Such explanations may account for the genesis and rather loose form of the *Memoir of a Brother*, but why expose this family document to a wider audience by means of publication? Hughes's position is that it is not only from the lives of famous people that valuable lessons can be learned. Especially in troubled times, the reading public should be reminded of "the reserve of strength and power which lies quietly at the nation's call, outside the whirl and din of public and fashionable life, and entirely ignored in the columns of the daily press." It is important to recognize that there are many, like George Hughes, who display "high culture, high courage, high principle, who are living their own quiet lives in every corner of the kingdom, from John o' Groat's to the Land's-End, bringing up their families in the love of God and their neighbour, and keeping the atmosphere around them clean, and pure and strong, by their example,—men who would come to the front, and might be relied on, in any serious national crisis" (*Memoir*, viii).

However, despite Hughes's repeated assurances in the preface and at intervals throughout the *Memoir* that George's life was exemplary, it is not always easy to see exactly how this is so. To be sure, he served as a model to Tom, especially during their boyhood and youth, and no doubt this fact biases him as a biographer; but there is much in George's story, even as it is recorded by his devoted younger brother, that cannot readily be reconciled with the claims that are made for it in this book.

Though George Hughes was a capable student and a gifted athlete, his career at school and college was by and large disappointing. He was dismissed from Rugby, under circumstances that are explained less than fully in the *Memoir*. At Oxford, George's sociability and especially his failure to keep visitors out of his rooms when he should have been studying interfered with his academic work and, according to the *Memoir,* prevented him from earning the first-class degree for which he had seemed destined.

Thomas Hughes does find much to praise in his brother's early life. Even though his agility and courage brought him many triumphs in sports and games, George "never neglected the real purpose of a schoolboy's life for them" (*Memoir,* 18–19). Not only a promising student, George was also a skillful writer and "had the pleasure of seeing himself in print" (*Memoir,* 29) in *Bentley's Miscellany,* an important periodical of the day, while still a pupil at Rugby. He was invariably honest and honorable. But some troubling aspects of his character also showed themselves during these years, and Thomas Hughes deals frankly with them. George's "easy-going" nature and "constitutional indolence" "led him to shirk trouble in small matters, and to leave things to manage themselves" (*Memoir,* 49). Chapter 3 is largely devoted to letters written by John Hughes in which he remonstrates with his son about such shortcomings, and most of the instructive features of this portion of the *Memoir* are to be found in these fatherly admonitions rather than in George's own activities or reflections. Thomas Hughes adds the advice that his brother's youthful disappointments and reverses should teach the next generation to make the most of their opportunities because "neither boys nor men *do* get second chances in this world" (*Memoirs,* 41).

There is no more overt blame of George in the remainder of the *Memoir*; on the contrary, Hughes goes out of his way to praise his brother on every possible occasion. Nevertheless, an objective reader is tempted to look to these early chapters for an explanation of George Hughes's lack of achievement in adult life and to question the allowances that Thomas Hughes seems eager to make for him.

Instead of taking up a career immediately after receiving his Oxford degree, George spends three years as a tutor at Harrow. Is this indolence or want of purpose? No; he is using those years to study modern languages, to engage in general reading, and to decide whether or not to enter the church. Having qualified as a barrister and become a Doctor of Civil Law, George travels to Italy rather than practicing his profession. Procrastination? No; he has suffered an eye injury that makes it impossible for him to work. When he does start work in the Ecclesiastical Courts, he stays only a few years. Lack of professional commitment? No; family obligations require his presence elsewhere, with his wife's ailing stepmother or with his dying father.

Hughes takes the view that George's abandonment of the law did not lead to a life of idleness. On the contrary, he worked hard at his responsibilities as a husband, a son, a brother, a father, and an uncle; he pursued literary and musical avocations; he traveled; he engaged in field sports; he farmed; he participated in the volunteer movement; he maintained a keen interest in public affairs; he served as a magistrate; he strove to educate the ignorant and succor the needy in his village. There was undeniably much that was admirable in these occupations and in the upright character that George Hughes brought to them.

On the other hand, it is clear that George found this kind of existence wanting by contrast with what he might have made of himself had he followed a different path: "he could never in all these years get the notion quite out of his head ... that he was not doing his fair share of work in the world, and was a useless kind of personage" (*Memoir*, 138). Though the word is not used in the *Memoir of a Brother*, Hughes does suggest that there is something close to heroism in a man who dedicates himself conscientiously to domestic and local duties even while lamenting that he is outside the mainstream of public life.

An inordinately large portion—the first eight chapters, or more than two-thirds—of the *Memoir of a Brother* is given over to George Hughes's boyhood and young manhood. Not until chapters 9 and 10 does Thomas Hughes attempt to do justice to the last twenty-one years of George's short life, but in the process he exacerbates problems that are characteristic of the book as a whole. He begins the ninth chapter, which he calls "Middle Life," by showing George as ready at last to work in his profession. After only a few lines about the law, he changes the subject; "his professional career was destined to be short and broken, and need not detain us. It is his home life with which we are concerned ..." (*Memoir*, 130). Beyond the fact that he married "in the autumn of 1852" (*Memoir*, 131), however, the chapter contains virtually nothing about his new family; not even the names of his wife and children are given. Chapter 10 does provide what its title promises: "Letters to His Boys." There are some twenty of these here, with very little commentary by Thomas Hughes to blend them into anything like a coherent whole—not the first time in the *Memoir of a Brother* that the biographer surrenders control of his narrative, indeed abandoning it altogether in favor of documents that are presented much as Hughes himself received them.[11]

By the time the reader reaches the eleventh and concluding chapter, he is likely to be puzzled about where Thomas Hughes is leading him. Hughes, too, it turns out from the opening words of that chapter, is dissatisfied with what he has written so far, but for a different reason. Presumably he knows most of what the baffled reader has been hoping in vain to learn about George and his significance; but he realizes that he has been confining himself to "the outer life" of his brother without adequately probing "that which underlies the outer life" (*Memoir*, 170), and he pledges to do what he can to make up for this deficiency in the rest of the book. That there is a significant relationship between material and spiritual existence is clear to this disciple of Carlyle, and he expresses his sense of the connection in language reminiscent of the "clothes-philosophy" of Carlyle's *Sartor Resartus*: "the one life will no doubt always be the visible expression of the other; just as the body is the garment in which the real man is clothed for his sojourn in time" (*Memoir*, 171). But, despite his best efforts, Hughes is unable to take us much beyond externals even in this "Conclusion." We are told what George Hughes had to say about the religious controversies of his age and how he behaved when he was in the presence of the dying or in charge of prayer meetings; but these are, after all, only outward signs of his inner religious nature, and "the real man" remains elusive.

It was probably a mistake for Hughes to consent to the publication of his *Memoir of a Brother*. In a work intended solely for circulation within the family, it might have been entirely appropriate for him to glorify George Hughes, and the awkwardness with which he handles his materials would doubtless have been overlooked. But in a book that was to be read by strangers, most of whom had never heard of George, a more dispassionate and penetrating psychological portrait, more coherently rendered from a consistent standpoint and providing more personal facts about the subject than his nephews and sons apparently required, would have been welcome.[12]

Memoir of Daniel Macmillan

Like the *Memoir* of George Hughes, the biography of Daniel Macmillan owes its existence to a brother's desire to do homage to a worthy man who died before his time, unable to realize his potential. But Macmillan's career, in contrast to George Hughes's, was clearly a success by any reasonable standard, having taken him in a relatively few years from humble Scottish origins to eminence and wealth in the highly competitive world of mid-Victorian publishing.

Hughes was of course aware that Macmillan's dramatic rise to fame and fortune was the stuff of readable biography, but there were other reasons why he accepted Alexander Macmillan's invitation to turn his brother's letters and diaries into a book. Personal allegiance was one such reason: as we have seen, Hughes and Daniel Macmillan were good friends. Moreover, Hughes felt that Macmillan possessed rare qualities that made him an admirable man whose life would prove richly instructive. In that respect, if in no others, he resembled both King Alfred and George Hughes.

In the first place, Macmillan displayed a large measure of heroism. For more than two decades he was in precarious health, suffering from a pulmonary complaint that Hughes never names, though it appears to have been tuberculosis. Beset with virtually constant illness, pain, and anxiety, Macmillan nevertheless applied himself resolutely to his duties "and retained to the last a joyousness and playfulness in his intercourse with his family and friends, which made it almost impossible to realise upon how frail a thread his life hung."[13]

Furthermore, in an age when publishers were turning from small-scale booksellers into large-scale commercial entrepreneurs—a transition in which he himself played an important role—Macmillan never allowed his sense of vocation to be swallowed up by purely business considerations. A voracious and perceptive reader though he had had little formal education, he venerated books and could never look on them as mere merchandise: he knew and loved the ones his firm dealt in, and he was deeply sensitive to the effect they would have on those who bought and read them. Long before he became a publisher, Macmillan wrote to a friend in Scotland who, like him at the time, was working in a bookshop:

Don't you know that you are cultivating good taste amongst the natives of Glasgow; helping to unfold a love of the beautiful among those who are slaves to the useful, or what they call the useful? I look on you as a great teacher or prophet, doing work just of the kind that God has appointed you to do.... We booksellers, if we are faithful to our task, are trying to destroy, and are helping to destroy, all kinds of confusion, and are aiding our great Taskmaster to reduce the world into order, and beauty, and harmony. (*Macmillan*, 116)

He retained this conviction to the end of his career.

Like his business dealings, Macmillan's personal life was always imbued with a powerful Christian commitment, but not until he was in his thirties was he able to rest easy in his faith. What most interested Hughes about Macmillan's long search for a satisfactory religion was that, unlike so many nineteenth-century Scots who threw off the stern Calvinism in which they had been reared, he continued to hold fast to "the central truth which gives all its strength and vitality to that system" (*Macmillan*, xi). Macmillan did not abandon his quest, even in an age when other thoughtful men and women came to believe they could no longer accept any form of Christianity. Having found the Baptist church he joined while living in Cambridge and the Congregational chapel he attended in London as unrewarding as Presbyterianism, he was finally drawn to a Broad Church kind of Anglicanism through the writings of F. D. Maurice and Augustus Hare, both of whom became his friends.

There was much in Daniel Macmillan's life and character, then, to make him a congenial subject for Hughes. His book delighted Alexander Macmillan,[14] and a hundred years after its publication the *Memoir of Daniel Macmillan* still conveys a striking picture of a remarkable man. But there is little depth to that picture, and even in its two dimensions it leaves some spaces blank or barely sketched in.

As usual in his biographies, Hughes quotes copiously from his subject's letters and journals. There can be no doubt about their intrinsic interest, especially when they record Macmillan's extensive reading and his insightful reactions to the ideas he encountered in books. Noteworthy, too, is the moving frankness with which he records his mental and spiritual agonies. For instance, in 1833, while job-hunting in London, he writes his brother William a letter taking up more than a dozen printed pages that gives a circumstantial description of his increasingly desperate wanderings from one prospective employer to another but also contains passages like this: " 'My mind was in the most restless state. I could not tell what made it so. Old sins kept stalking before me. I was miserable. I walked about the streets, but saw nothing. I was jostled on the streets, yet I saw no face that I cared about, scarcely noticed those who pressed on me. The strangeness of everything increased my misery. I prayed. I tried to pray. I thought. I tried to think, my mind was a strange whirlpool. I could look at nothing. I could only weep, and try to pray' " (*Macmillan*,

42). In his distress and agitation, Macmillan frequently turns to prayer. On one occasion, in 1834, he beseeches God to keep him " 'from fretting—from being tossed and disturbed by proud and wicked thoughts. . . . O Lord, if it be possible, if it be Thy will, grant that, by some means or other, I may be delivered from this load. If *that* is not Thy will, enable me to endure. It is easier to talk of patience than to be patient. May I really be patient' " (*Macmillan*, 65).

Hughes has chosen deliberately to let Daniel Macmillan speak for himself in passages such as these. "Readers will judge, each for himself," he says in one place, "how far this journal has a true ring about it" (*Macmillan*, 62). That may be so, but those same readers would have welcomed a fuller account by Macmillan's biographer of the origin and significance of his subject's confessions. Why did Macmillan find it so difficult to be at peace with himself?

There is at least one other aspect of the darker side of Macmillan's character that is left unexplored. Hughes mentions his "natural vehemence and fiery temper" (*Macmillan*, 6), but provides only one example, from early in Macmillan's life: his indignant reaction to an unjust reprimand from the Irvine bookseller and bookbinder to whom he was apprenticed at the age of ten. There are frequent references to the persistence of this hot temper into Macmillan's manhood— for example, Macmillan himself speaks of " 'a needless vehemence of all occasions' " (*Macmillan*, 180) in an 1850 letter to his fiancée —but when he is shown in his dealings with other people all we see is an exceptionally civil and forbearing man.

In the one chapter he devotes to Macmillan's "Marriage and Home Life," too, Hughes refrains from interpretation and commentary. With some reluctance, he acknowledges that a biographer is obliged to glance at his subject's relationship with his family, but raises a "difficult and delicate" question as to "how far the veil can be drawn back so as to let the man be seen in those relations which most shrewdly test his manhood, without pandering to idle curiosity, or uncovering things too sacred for the casual eye of strangers."[15] Because in the present case there is "nothing but what is pure and of good report, and the principal actors have passed from amongst us," he answers the question reassuringly by saying that "the light may be let in freely" (*Macmillan*, 178). Except for a few transitional passages, however, the rest of this chapter, some twenty-six pages, consists entirely of excerpts from letters and journal entries. Once again, it is the subject rather than the biographer who speaks, and everything he says is taken at face value.

It was almost inevitable in the Victorian age that the author of a commissioned biography would be excessively discreet, especially if he was as fond of his subject as Hughes clearly was of Macmillan. But the need to take such a cautious approach should not excuse him from the task of shaping his materials with some care, a task Hughes fails to perform in the *Memoir of Daniel Macmillan*.

Life and Times of Peter Cooper

Hughes's next venture of this kind showed that his customary circumspection as a biographer could not always be counted on to gain his work the approval of his subject's closest relatives.

Peter Cooper died on April 4, 1883, a venerated public benefactor. The following year, his son-in-law, Abram S. Hewitt, asked Hughes to write Cooper's life, and Hughes readily agreed, not only because he admired Cooper but also because he and Hewitt had been friends since their first meeting in London in 1867, three years before Hughes became acquainted with Cooper himself. With the help of Hewitt and others who had been close to Cooper, Hughes worked on the book for over a year, completing it by the end of 1885. However, Cooper's daughter, Amelia Hewitt, considered Hughes's treatment of her father to be insufficiently reverential and ordered him to stop publication. Only fifty copies were printed; Hughes was allowed to keep a few, and the rest were shipped over to New York, where they were stored first in the basement of the Cooper home on Lexington Avenue and later at the Cooper Union. Some were subsequently released to American libraries.[16]

A century later, it is possible to understand what Amelia Hewitt objected to in the *Life and Times of Peter Cooper* but difficult to agree that she showed good judgment in having the biography suppressed. Hughes obviously had the greatest respect for "the old philanthropist of New York, of whom, as of the Roman emperor, it may be said, that he found his capital a city of brick, and left her a city of marble." To be sure, he could not bring himself to call Cooper "the typical hero whom our English-speaking race desires just now to honour," possibly because other preoccupations kept Cooper from playing much of a part on the national stage until he was over eighty, and when he did run for president in 1876 it was on the eccentric platform of the Greenback party. As a mark of his high esteem, however, Hughes quickly added that "whenever that hero appears, he will have much in common, both in aim and spirit," with Cooper.[17] An enormously wealthy man, Cooper never valued material possessions for their own sake, preferring to lavish his money on worthy public causes. Hughes could only approve, and in the *Life and Times of Peter Cooper* he frequently makes clear that he does, most heartily. Moreover, Cooper was an idealist after Hughes's own heart, a man gifted with the practical intellect and resolute will to turn his visions into realities despite opposition and difficulties of all kinds. In short, he was a fighter, in the sense in which all heroes have to be fighters.

Though he says less than he might about Cooper's industrial ventures, Hughes does tell the reader of the *Life and Times of Peter Cooper* a great deal about his subject's diverse activities. An inventor from boyhood, Cooper built the first steam locomotive used on an American railroad, the *Tom Thumb*. He was active in New York municipal government, making especially notable contributions in the areas of public education and water supply, and leading the fight against the corruption of Tammany Hall through the Citizens' Association, which he helped to found and served as president. He took a prominent role in the laying of the first Atlantic cable. Though initially an advocate of compromise with the South, he worked tirelessly for the Northern cause during the Civil War. But what probably endeared Cooper to Hughes more than any other of his many achievements was his establishment and generous support of the Cooper Union for the Advancement of Science and Art as "an institution designed to supply great opportunities for instruction and rational recreation to wage-workers" (*Cooper*, 154), much as the Working Men's College had been doing in London.

More than he did in writing about George Hughes or Daniel Macmillan, Hughes allows his warm, if sometimes amused, affection for his subject to appear in this biography. No doubt remembering his own first visit, he describes the contagious zest with which the elderly Cooper rushed foreigners around to see the attractions of New York—including, of course, the Cooper Union—driving "his buggy through the most crowded parts of the city" (*Cooper*, 234) with carefree abandon. Hughes is a sympathetic friend rather than a mischievous caricaturist when he depicts Cooper, who suffered for forty years from a bone ailment that made it difficult for him to sit comfortably, carrying a rubber cushion around to the many meetings he was required to attend—hardly a heroic picture, though in its own way an endearing one.

Probably it was the fact that Hughes for once allowed his characteristic playfulness to appear in a biography that offended Amelia Hewitt. It is necessary to reiterate that Hughes's attitude toward Cooper was predominantly one of profound respect and to point out that all of the human touches in the *Life and Times of Peter Cooper*, including the story about the rubber cushion, are taken directly from Cooper's own unpublished "Reminiscences," on which Hughes drew freely in writing his book.[18]

Cooper was very matter-of-fact about his own reverses, and as his biographer Hughes does not flinch from telling the truth about them. It was from the "Reminiscences" that Hughes learned that Cooper had been unusually accident-prone from childhood, so much so that it was a wonder that he survived into adult life more or less unscarred. It was in the "Reminiscences," too, that Cooper described those of his projects that miscarried; reproducing long stretches of Cooper's own accounts, Hughes discusses these failures as well as the spectacular successes, making it quite clear that the latter clearly outweighed the former in number and importance and that Cooper is to be prized far above those lesser men of limited vision who do not fail only because they never dare to attempt anything out of the ordinary.

It may be argued that it would have been prudent for Hughes to be less honest about Cooper in the *Life* than Cooper was about himself in the "Reminiscences." In any case, Hughes's copious use of Cooper's own words sometimes obscures the truth even while it appears to reveal the facts. For example, when writing about Cooper's grandiloquently phrased but really quite vague religious views, which baffle him, or about Cooper's insistence that currency should not be convertible into gold, which alarms him, he does not attempt to subject Cooper's ideas to any sort of analysis. Rather he prefers "to put the best materials for forming a judgment fairly before [his] readers, leaving them to draw their own conclusions" (*Cooper*, 137) regarding the matter of religion, and "to place our hero's views and contentions fairly before our readers without note or comment beyond this" (*Cooper*, 193) regarding the matter of paper money. Primary materials like unpublished autobiographies and speeches have their value to a biographer, but he should use them creatively rather than abdicating his authority to them.

In his treatment of Cooper's private life, Hughes works from the same principle and follows the same procedure we observed in the *Memoir of Daniel Macmillan*. He maintains that "unless a man's home life has been such that contact with it will send the reader back to his own fireside a gentler, braver, brighter man, it should be scrupulously let alone" (*Cooper*, 221). In Cooper's case, as in Macmillan's, there is nothing to hide. But rather than reaching his own conclusions, Hughes relies on Cooper's "Reminiscences," saying that "from those parts of them which relate to his family and home a few extracts will be enough for our purpose" (*Cooper*, 222).

These "extracts" tell a melancholy story, one that was common enough in the nineteenth century and one to which Hughes himself as a father had been no stranger. Cooper's first four children died in infancy or soon after; though he recounts in horrifying detail the story of a daughter's blindness and a clumsy surgeon's brutal method of trying to deal with it, Cooper is laconic about the deaths themselves. Hughes does add the comment that this "is a brave record of sorrows bravely and silently borne. In the whole of the *Reminiscences* there is no whining or rebellious note, and no despondency" (*Cooper*, 228). The reader is likely to share Hughes's admiration for Cooper's courage in bereavement, but he looks in vain to the *Life and Times of Peter Cooper* for any explanation of the man's stoic nature or any attempt to link this to his worldly successes.

Nor is this the only occasion when Hughes fails to draw inferences from the evidence he supplies in such abundant detail. It is his thesis in chapter 2, "Forefathers," for instance, that—to put it as kindly as possible—Cooper misrepresented his origins, frequently claiming that, like the men who came to the Cooper Union to study, he had started out in the working class. Hughes demonstrates that Cooper was at best stretching the truth in making this claim and certainly does not condemn him for it; but neither does he ask why Cooper might have wanted to engage in this innocent deception. Clearly Peter Cooper was no Josiah Bounderby, the loathsome industrialist in Dickens's *Hard Times* who boasted, falsely, that he had been born in a ditch and raised himself by his bootstraps; it would have been well for Hughes to rule out such a reading of the myth about himself that Cooper created.

We are given a great deal of information, probably more than we want or need, in the *Life and Times of Peter Cooper*, but the complexity of the versatile genius who is the subject of that biography tends to elude us.

James Fraser

In writing his next biography—*James Fraser, Second Bishop of Manchester: A Memoir, 1818–1885,* to give it its full title—Hughes had at least as much material at his disposal as he had ever had to work with in his previous efforts in this line. Fraser died in October 1885; early the next year, having persuaded Hughes to do the book, Mrs. Fraser turned over to him " '15 vols. (about 6 inches thick each) of his addresses, speeches, rows with mad parsons etc. which [she had] collected and which with other materials such as letters and reports on Education in the U.S. etc. fill a big trunk.' "[19]

As usual, Hughes made extensive use of such papers, quoting copiously from Fraser's letters in particular and often letting them tell his story. Nevertheless, *James Fraser* is a more compelling piece of work than Hughes's other biographies of men he had known. Not only was there a good deal more to say about someone who had had a long and distinguished career than about George Hughes and Daniel Macmillan, both of whom had died in early middle age, but in writing Fraser's life Hughes was not as constrained as he had been in designing a book about his own brother for the edification of his own sons and nephews, and his affinities with Fraser were much closer than his ties to Macmillan or, especially, Peter Cooper.

Hughes shared Fraser's West Country, public-school, and Oxford background. Holding religious and social views that were remarkably similar, Hughes the lawyer and Fraser the churchman often espoused the same causes, using Parliament—the House of Commons in Hughes's case, the House of Lords in Fraser's—as one of their forums. It is worth noting, too, that some of Fraser's personal traits were strongly reminiscent of important aspects of Hughes's character. We cannot be surprised that the two men were friends for over forty years.

Hughes takes the reader step by step through a meticulous account of Fraser's rise from an ordinary boyhood to national prominence, making clear at every opportunity his admiration for Fraser's devotion to church and people, his forthrightness, his capacity for hard work, his administrative ability, his integrity, and his self-deprecating sense of humor.

One quality in Fraser that Hughes finds especially appealing is his courage and perseverance when locked in conflict with powerful or devious adversaries. He never shrank from a challenge to his authority or to the principles of the Church of England as he understood them, even when his refusal to countenance inappropriate behavior exposed him to considerable professional risk. Just as Fraser had prevailed against a blustering squire when he was the young rector of the Wiltshire parish of Cholderton, so as Bishop of Manchester he would brook no insubordination from plausible clergymen who insisted on diverging from middle-of-the-road Anglicanism in the direction of either ritualism or Unitarianism. As far from a "muscleman" or a bully as any man could be, Fraser was a fighter in a sense of which Hughes heartily approved.

Feeling the same indifference to abstruse biblical scholarship and the same aversion to doctrinal hair-splitting as Hughes, Fraser also resembled his friend and biographer in viewing the Church of England as a comprehensive national institution that should cater to believers of all persuasions and move with the times while holding fast to its enduring essence. He characterized himself accurately and justly in the letter he wrote Prime Minister Gladstone accepting his appointment as Bishop of Manchester:

I never was, and never could be, a partisan. Even when seeing my way most clearly I am always inclined to give credit to others whose views may be different from my own for equal clearness of vision, certainly for equal honesty of purpose. As little of a dogmatist as it is possible to be, I yet see the use, and, indeed the necessity, of dogma; but I have always wished to narrow, rather than to extend, its field, because the less peremptorily articles of faith are imposed or defined the more hope there is of eliciting agreements rather than differences. Especially have I been anxious to see the Church adapt herself more genially and trustfully to the intellectual aspirations of the age, not standing aloof in a timorous or hostile attitude from the spirit of scientific inquiry, but rather endeavouring (as is her function) to temper its ardour with the spirit of reverence and godly fear. And, finally, my great desire will be, without disguising my own opinions, or wishing one set of minds to understand me in one sense and another in the opposite, to throw myself on *the heart* of the whole diocese, of the laity as well as of the clergy, of those who differ from the Church as well as those who conform to her.[20]

This was exactly the sort of credo that Hughes would wish a bishop of the national church to hold, and Fraser rigorously lived up to it during the decade and a half that he occupied his high office.

Addressing a congregation of working men in Trinity Church, Salford, Fraser declared, " 'I regret bitterly that churches, not only in Manchester but all over England, and I fear chapels also, are too much in the possession of the well-dressed, the comfortable, and the well-to-do' " (*Fraser*, 193). He believed, as did Hughes, that the Church of England would betray its exalted mission if it failed to carry the word of God to the working class or to minister to the needs of the poor, compassionately rather than condescendingly. The fact that as bishop he enjoyed great popularity in a diocese where both nonconformity and unbelief claimed wide allegiance indicates to Hughes that Fraser's words and deeds persuaded the lower orders of his unimpeachable honesty. He was too honest, indeed, to sympathize with them when they acted foolishly, but neither was he an apologist for the employers of labor. As Fraser himself put it, " 'I am no lover of the principles of trades unionism, but they have been forced on the working classes by the inequitable use of the power of capital' " (*Fraser*, 225). Both sides perceived Fraser as notably fair-minded, and for this reason he was on several occasions called on to arbitrate labor disputes.

Like Hughes, Fraser was troubled by the adversarial stance characteristic of trade unions and saw much greater promise for a future free of industrial conflict and materialistic greed in the cooperative movement. While serving on the Commission on the Employment of Children, Young Persons, and Women in Agriculture in 1867, he was much impressed by what he saw of an experiment in cooperative farming, and in his later years he became a strong ally of the movement, taking part in its meetings and making its case to his colleagues in the church.

Clearly, James Fraser's life and opinions evoked Hughes's profound sympathy. It must be said, however, that, though his treatment of Fraser is more penetrating than his depiction of George Hughes or Daniel Macmillan or Peter Cooper, Hughes does miss some opportunities to explore in greater depth certain of Fraser's attitudes, perhaps for the very reason that they so closely resembled his own.

For example, Fraser believed as strongly as did Hughes that the Church of England must reach out to all Christians and that the ceremonial excesses of ritualism—" 'incense, lighted candles, eucharistic

vestments, the eastward position, the mixed chalice, and wafer bread' "
—must be discouraged, in large part because they would offend the
nonconformists whom the Broad Church was trying to attract. " 'To
make such things vital is the height of human folly' " (Fraser, 241),
Fraser warned.

On the other hand, Fraser was attracted by some of the elaborate
trappings of High Church worship, especially as a young man. He
was unmoved by a service he attended at Rochester Cathedral in 1844,
complaining in a letter to his mother that it was " 'not to be com-
pared with the style of that at Exeter—the minor canon reads, instead
of chanting—which mars the effect' " (Fraser, 35). At Cholderton,
Fraser preached in a surplice rather than a plain gown and only
discontinued the practice when some of the more influential members
of his congregation complained. The physical appearance of a church
mattered a good deal to him; as he wrote a friend from Cholderton,
" 'One does not wish to attribute to externals more weight than they
deserve; but with me there is always a heavy pressure on my spirits,
quite crushing all attempts to be devotional, when I am in a dilapi-
dated, dark-green, square-pewed church; while all seems in harmony,
and one's soul can soar a little, when one worships in such a church
as I have got here' " (Fraser, 97).

There seems to be an inconsistency here. Perhaps a certain ro-
manticism colored Fraser's early religious outlook and he outgrew
it with age, or else he learned to keep it in check as he rose in the
church. It is possible, too, that Fraser never really reconciled his High
Church leanings with his Broad Church pronouncements. Some attempt at explanation by his biographer seems called for, but none is
provided, probably because Hughes—even less of a thinker than
Fraser, and even more of an advocate of compromise between ex-
tremes in the Church of England—saw no difficulty in giving emotional assent to a religious position that many would brand as intellectually indefensible.

Nor does Hughes comment on the striking frequency and intensity
with which Fraser professed his belief that he was unworthy of
ecclesiastical preferment: when he was about to be ordained a deacon,
immediately after he became a priest, when he was offered the
bishopric of Calcutta, when he was told that he had been second in
line for the bishopric of Salisbury, when Gladstone invited him to
succeed A. P. Stanley as Dean of Westminster (Fraser, 47, 50, 140,
161–62, 317). He accepted the bishopric of Manchester only after

considerable soul-searching, and it took him some time to get used to the position. Two years after his appointment, he wrote a friend: " 'I can't think how I let my friends persuade me that I was fit to be a Bishop. I don't say that I am unhappy, but I am dissatisfied with myself; the work is above my power, and I feel myself not half good or holy enough for such an office as I have to fill' " (*Fraser*, 201). Were such declarations signs of genuine humility or merely pro forma expressions of modesty? If they were sincere, which seems likely in view of everything else we learn about the man, what qualities in Fraser enabled him to overcome these deeply held feelings of his own inadequacy? We are not told in *James Fraser*. Once again—even in this longest of his biographies, crammed with primary information— Hughes declines to supply conclusions that he is in a far better position than his readers to draw.

David Livingstone

Whereas Hughes had grown up with his brother George and known Daniel Macmillan, Peter Cooper, and James Fraser, he seems to have had no personal contact with the subject of his last biography, though he was of course aware of David Livingstone's immense reputation.[21] On Livingstone's return from Africa in the winter of 1856– 57, he was feted as a national hero, and his *Missionary Travels and Researches in South Africa* (1857) became a best seller a few months after the enthusiastic reception accorded *Tom Brown's School Days*.[22] Livingstone's *Cambridge Lectures* were published the following year and his *Narrative of an Expedition to the Zambesi* in 1865, and these books added to his fame. So did the appearance of Henry Morton Stanley's *How I Found Livingstone* in 1872 and of Livingstone's *Last Journals* in 1874. In the latter year his remains were brought back to England from what is now Zambia, where he had died on May 1, 1873, for interment in Westminster Abbey in a moving and well-publicized ceremony.

An official biography of Livingstone came out in 1880. Commissioned by the Livingstone family, *The Personal Life of David Livingstone* by William Garden Blaikie drew heavily on unpublished documents, much as Hughes's *Memoir of a Brother, Memoir of Daniel Macmillan, Life and Times of Peter Cooper*, and *James Fraser* had done. Among the many appreciative readers of Blaikie's work was Hughes's publisher, Alexander Macmillan, who had known Livingstone,[23] and who suggested to Hughes that he initiate Macmillan's "English Men of Action" series with a brief volume about the renowned explorer.

An examination of *David Livingstone* makes clear why Hughes agreed to Macmillan's suggestion even though he knew relatively little about Livingstone or Africa.[24] For Livingstone, in Hughes's estimation, was another of those heroic figures who persist and prevail against incredible odds in order to do God's will in the world: spreading the Christian faith, healing the sick, extending human knowledge, and battling against slavery, which Livingstone abhorred as much as Hughes.

Having gone to Africa in 1841 as a medical missionary determined to take the Gospel where no white man had ever gone before, Livingstone traveled into and around the interior under appalling conditions, contending with the climate, the terrain, wild animals (he was mauled and nearly killed by a lion in 1843, and his body still bore the scars thirty years later when it was prepared for burial), disease, hunger, treacherous natives, hostile Boers, and suspicious Portuguese and African slavers, not to mention jealous fellow missionaries and unreliable European companions. Nevertheless, in addition to carrying out the work he had gone to Africa to do, he made numerous geographical discoveries that changed the map of the continent: Lake Ngami, the Zambezi River, Victoria Falls, and Lake Nyasa, to mention only a few of the best known. Unlike most earlier missionaries in his willingness to accept the Africans on their own terms rather than looking down on them as benighted heathens, Livingstone was a serious student of ethnology, linguistics, and comparative religion; a trained physician who was keenly interested in natural history, he recorded many valuable scientific observations as well as refining the practice of tropical medicine. Through his eloquent denunciation of the African slave trade, he helped to bring about its abolition; and through his vision of humane and productive economic arrangements that would benefit Africans and Europeans alike as much as slavery had harmed both groups, he laid the foundation for the commercial development of much of the continent.

By the time Hughes began working on his book in 1887, there was already in print a wealth of material by and about Livingstone to help him overcome his unfamiliarity with his latest subject— material he followed closely and from which he quoted extensively, even though the format of the series to which *David Livingstone* was a contribution demanded terseness. In falling back on old habits in this way, Hughes was making a serious mistake. In the five hundred pages of *The Personal Life of David Livingstone*, Blaikie had had ample scope to go into detail about Livingstone's nearly three decades of peregrinations all over southern and central Africa and to weave excerpts from various documents into his narrative. Having only two hundred pages at his disposal, by contrast, Hughes was faced with a choice: either summarize and synthesize, or else inundate the reader with specifics and regale him with quotations. Hughes chose the latter course.[25]

David Livingstone is written with Hughes's usual verve, and it does offer a concise, if not always totally accurate, account of Livingstone's achievements. But the abundance of unfamiliar names—of persons, places, and tribes—crowded into such a restricted space makes for confusion; and though the quotations from Livingstone, and in the appropriate places from Stanley, often have an attractive immediacy, there are occasions when they lack apparent relevance or when Hughes fails to capitalize on them as he might. Surprisingly, too, there is remarkably little of Hughes's customary preaching in the book. Most of his comments on Livingstone's significance as a Christian hero are made in passing, and there are no extended sermons such as those that appear in *Alfred the Great*, which—however jarring they might seem—do articulate a theme and thereby serve to hold that work together.

Two chapters, one from the first half of *David Livingstone* and the other from the second, display typical strengths and weaknesses of Hughes's book.

Chapter 8 deals with the initial thirty-three months of Livingstone's Zambezi expedition at the start of his second stay in Africa, from his leaving England in March 1858 until the sinking of the steam launch *Ma-Robert* above Sena in December 1860. (Hughes's dates in this chapter are off by a year: he has Livingstone setting out from Liverpool in 1859 and the *Ma-Robert* running aground in 1861). It begins promisingly by contrasting Livingstone's honored position at the time with the precarious footing on which he had carried out his earlier explorations and by attempting to draw the appropriate moral from the adventures that are to follow: "God's great workers," constantly beset as they are by "the powers of evil," can never count on an easy "repetition of that first triumphant success."[26]

The rest of the chapter, however, is considerably less clear-cut.

Livingstone leads the expedition up the Zambezi River as far as the Kebrabasa Rapids, then up the Shire to Lake Nyasa, and up the Zambezi again to Victoria Falls and Sesheke, with a side trip to Linyanti to retrieve supplies he left there several years earlier. Hughes attempts to tell this complicated and eventful story, which involves a large number of key characters, in fourteen pages; it took Blaikie forty, and one very useful modern study, George Seaver's *David Livingstone* (1957), devotes sixty-seven pages and three chapters to this phase of Livingstone's travels. In Hughes's account, the names and incidents go by too swiftly for ready comprehension. Moreover, he omits any reference to the less heroic aspects of Livingstone's character that were often manifested on this dangerous journey. Even Blaikie in his authorized biography alludes to Livingstone's "intense irritability of temper";[27] Seaver is very explicit about it, as he is about Livingstone's quarrels with some of his white associates, including his brother Charles, which Hughes also leaves out.

The few relatively leisurely stretches of Hughes's *David Living-stone* can be as unilluminating as the more hurried chapters. His fifteenth chapter depicts Livingstone's five-month wait at Unyanyembe, east of Lake Tanganyika, for the porters Stanley had promised to send him from Zanzibar so that he could resume his explorations. In the first paragraph, Hughes says that, though Livingstone was "sorely tried by the delay, all the work which could be done on a halt went on as usual. No correspondence or observations were neglected which could forward any branch of his work, scientific, philanthropical, or religious, and every available resource, such as his few books afforded, used to the utmost" (*Livingstone*, 165). He then goes on to give over the remaining eleven pages almost entirely to extracts from Livingstone's journal, virtually without commentary of his own. As Hughes presents them, there is no discernible significance to entries like that for April 15, 1872, which reads in its entirety: " 'Hung up sounding line on poles one fathom apart, and tarred it' " (*Living-stone*, 166). The one for June 24 of the same year, on the other hand, is full of implications, but Hughes ventures no conclusions as to what it might reveal about Livingstone's complicated mind.

"The medical education has led me to a continual tendency to suspend the judgment. What a state of blessedness it would have been had I possessed the dead certainty of the homoeopathists, and as soon as I found Lakes Bangweolo, Moero, and Kamalondo pouring their waters down the great central valley, bellowed out, 'Hurrah! Eureka!' and got home in firm and honest belief that I had settled it, and no mistake. Instead of that I am even now not cocksure that I have not been following down what may after all be the Congo." (*Livingstone*, 170)[28]

Blaikie needs only six pages and Seaver seven to cover the same period; both of them use journal entries, too, but manage to give a much more coherent sense than Hughes of the meaning of this pause in Livingstone's life, which was then rapidly nearing its close.

Hughes's handling of the dramatic encounter between Livingstone and Stanley and of their subsequent relationship also leaves much to be desired. He has Stanley turning up at Ujiji without preparation of any kind, simply quoting from Livingstone's journal for October 24, 1871.[29] It is Blaikie who says of that meeting, in words that Hughes might have used but did not, that it "was as unlikely an occurrence as could have happened, and, along with many of the earlier events in Livingstone's life, serves to show how wonderfully an Unseen Hand shaped and guarded his path."[30] As Blaikie and subsequent biographers make clear, Stanley and Livingstone were alike only in their indomitable courage; but despite the many and important differences between them, Stanley soon came to feel something like veneration for Livingstone. Hughes, instead of launching into a Carlylean disquisition, merely says that after a few weeks in Livingstone's company Stanley's "manly admiration had grown into enthusiasm and hero-worship" (*Livingstone*, 152), and then relies largely on Stanley's words in *How I Found Livingstone* to explain the attraction.

When Hughes does comment on his material, he sometimes fails to probe deeply enough. On what turned out to be his last birthday, March 19, 1873, the sixty-year-old Livingstone wrote in his journal: "Thanks to the Almighty Preserver of men for sparing me thus far on the journey of life. Can I hope for ultimate success? So many obstacles have arisen. Let no Satan prevail over me, Oh! my good Lord Jesus."[31] Hughes quotes this, not quite accurately, and then goes on to say, "A feeling which no one would call morbid, but for which it is difficult to find the precise phrase, undoubtedly grew upon him in these last months, that he was engaged in a personal encounter with a personal power of evil, in which death on the road would mean defeat" (*Livingstone*, 192–93). The matter was not quite that simple. Modern investigators have seen a "morbid" side to Living-

stone, even in his religious hopes and fears; and it is not necessary
to be a twentieth-century debunker of Victorian hero-figures to recognize that he was certainly a far more complex and probably a considerably less attractive man than Hughes's brief biography of him
would suggest.[32]

In the preface to his *Eminent Victorians* (1918), Lytton Strachey
speaks scathingly of recent English biography. "With us, the most
delicate and humane of all the branches of the art of writing has
been relegated to the journeymen of letters; we do not reflect that
it is perhaps as difficult to write a good life as to live one." He condemns the works of his predecessors for "their ill-digested masses of
material, their slipshod style, their tone of tedious panegyric, their
lamentable lack of selection, of detachment, of design."[33]
Strachey was being patently and even deliberately unfair, but two
things are clear. First, much Victorian and Edwardian biography was
guilty as charged; and, second, Thomas Hughes, who was certainly
a "journeyman of letters," did not rise above the general level of
his contemporaries in the writing of biography. In fact, his longer
works in that form—the *Life and Times of Peter Cooper* and *James
Fraser*—fall short of such significant achievements as Stanley's in
The Life and Correspondence of Thomas Arnold or John Forster's
in *The Life of Charles Dickens* (1872–74); whereas his briefer biographies lack the pithiness and critical insight to be found in the better
volumes in Macmillan's "English Men of Letters" series, such as Leslie
Stephen's *George Eliot* (1902).
But the shortcomings to which we have been pointing in this chapter must not be allowed to obscure the attractions that these six out-
dated volumes can still afford. They remain readable, they are full
of fascinating information about their gifted subjects, and—perhaps
of greatest importance—they tell us a great deal about Hughes that
is worth knowing for the light it sheds on his more famous work.

Chapter Six

Conclusion

After the first chapter, this study has sought to explicate the principal writings of Thomas Hughes. If at times it has seemed to stray from this aim into discussions of the man and his views about the world he lived in, there has been good reason for such a blurring of our focus.

As we have noted, Hughes never regarded himself as primarily an author. The fame he won as a consequence of the immense popularity of *Tom Brown's School Days* came as a complete surprise to him; even that novel was written from motives that had little to do with simply telling a good story, let alone painstakingly crafting a well-wrought piece of fiction. Hughes was essentially a preacher, one who could not help laying bare his character and personality as well as his convictions, so that in any consideration of his work it is even more difficult than usual—impossible, in fact—to divorce the "form" from the "content" of a piece of literature or to disregard the writer's intentions. That "content" and those intentions have done much to damage Hughes's reputation in the second half of the twentieth century.

We still read the novels and nonfictional prose of a number of Hughes's mid- and late-Victorian contemporaries, but most of his large output seems to have sunk without a trace. Even the present status of *Tom Brown's School Days* is questionable. Unlike Dickens's *Little Dorrit* and Trollope's *Barchester Towers*, both of which were also published in 1857, it is seldom taught in courses dealing with the nineteenth-century British novel; during the entire decade of the 1970s, the annual bibliographies of criticism and scholarship published in the journal *Victorian Studies* listed only two brief articles about it but scores about the fiction of Dickens, Trollope, and a half-dozen others. If such has been the fate of a novel that a respected periodical referred to less than a year after its publication as "a work which everybody has read, or means to read,"[1] and that was regarded as a minor classic for generations, it should not surprise us that Hughes's other writings have suffered even worse neglect.

The ideas embodied in those writings are anything but fashionable today. Even in his own lifetime, he was challenged again and again for trying to strike precarious balances between conservatism and innovation; given the present state of, say, labor relations or religion in his own country and everywhere else in the western world, his advocacy of Christian Socialism and a national church seems even more quixotic now than it did a century and more ago. *Tom Brown's School Days*, still his best-known work, has suffered for other reasons over which Hughes had little or no control. In the nineteenth century, Matthew Arnold was not the only reader who faulted it for conveying a misleading impression of what an English public school was or ought to be, an impression that was especially dangerous because of the novel's great popularity; in our own age, that kind of educational institution is almost beyond the comprehension of most American readers and condemned as elitist and class-bound by many of Hughes's compatriots. Especially in England, the more derisive recent comments about his quintessentially public-school novel seem to be based more on political than literary grounds.[2]

As far as Victorian nonfictional prose is concerned, it may be argued that the views of, for example, Thomas Carlyle are even more inimical to modern values than those of Thomas Hughes, and yet interest in Carlyle has, if anything, increased in recent years. So it has; but, for all their faults, Carlyle's works coruscate with a gnarled eloquence, and they grow out of a more or less coherent and profound spiritual vision. Hughes could bask in that light, but he himself was unable to shed anything like it. Similar comparisons could also be made, to Hughes's disadvantage, with such contemporaries of his as John Stuart Mill, John Henry Newman, and John Ruskin. We come back to the indivisibility of "form" and "content."

What, then, can justify devoting a whole book to Thomas Hughes as an author? For one thing, it is quite impossible to overlook the work of someone who wrote so much and so seriously and who was so widely admired for so many years by a public that was arguably the most demanding in the history of English literary taste. Also, for anyone who can set aside contemporary cynicism and prejudice Hughes remains an immensely attractive figure: principled, altruistic, ardently dedicated to making life better. His compassion extended to all men and women, including sweated laborers at home and black slaves overseas; his vision of a unified society reached beyond his own country to other English-speaking nations and ultimately the whole world. That he had shortcomings—impracticality, impulsiveness, a lack of political deftness, a mind that was less than first-rate—only makes him appear more human, not less appealing. To read his works is to come to know this man.

The works themselves merit more attention than they have recently received. As the preceding chapters have tried to show, even the most flawed of them retain an undeniable interest. That they remain approachable, even by a public that lacks information about or sympathy with Hughes, is shown by the success of the film and television versions of *Tom Brown's School Days*.[3] To provide such information and to induce such sympathy for the benefit of those who wish to read Thomas Hughes's works with understanding and enjoyment has been the principal purpose of this study.

Notes and References

Chapter One

1. Asa Briggs, *Victorian People* (Chicago, 1955), p. 149.

2. In 1890 Hughes began writing a memoir to be called *Early Memories for the Children*. Though never finished, it was printed "For Private Circulation Only" in 1899, three years after his death. Virtually identical with the *Early Memories*, Hughes's "Fragments of Autobiography" were published in three installments in the *Cornhill Magazine*, n.s. 58 (March 1925):280–89; (April 1925):472–78; and (May 1925): 563–72.

3. This is the date given in reference works like the *Dictionary of National Biography* and that Hughes considered his birthday. However, Catherine K. Firman infers from his father's manuscript diary that Hughes was actually born on October 18. See her "The Squire of Donnington Priory," *Notes and Queries*, n.s. 13 (May 1966):183.

4. *True Manliness*, ed. E. E. Brown (Boston, 1880), p. viii. This is a volume of extracts from Hughes's writings containing a fifteen-page autobiographical letter to James Russell Lowell.

5. Eugene L. Williamson, Jr., *The Liberalism of Thomas Arnold* (University: University of Alabama Press, 1964), pp. 223–27.

6. David Newsome, *Godliness & Good Learning* (London, 1961), p. 41.

7. T. W. Bamford, *Thomas Arnold* (London: Cresset, 1960), p. 179.

8. "Fifty Years Ago: A Layman's Address to Rugby School," repr. in *The Manliness of Christ* (London: Macmillan, 1894), pp. 191, 194.

9. Rowland E. Protheroe, *The Life and Correspondence of Arthur Penrhyn Stanley, D.D.* (London: John Murray, 1893), 1:68.

10. *True Manliness*, pp. xi–xii.

11. Torben Christensen, *Origin and History of Christian Socialism* (Aarhus: Universitetsforlaget, 1962), p. 69.

12. J. M. Ludlow, "Thomas Hughes and Septimus Hansard. A Sequel," *Economic Review* 6 (July 1896):299.

13. The two most authoritative historians of the movement, Christensen (see note 11) and Charles E. Raven in *Christian Socialism 1848–54* (London: Macmillan, 1920), agree that its life span was only six years. However, the ideals of Christian Socialism and the term itself survived

well into the twentieth century, influencing churchmen and politicians, especially some early members of the British Labour party.

14. Quoted in Edward C. Mack and W. H. G. Armytage, *Thomas Hughes* (London, 1952), p. 57.

15. "Milton and the Swedish Lord," *Ainsworth's Magazine*, 2 (November 1842):451.

16. *True Manliness*, p. xviii.

17. It was published in *Macmillan's Magazine* 5 (January 1862): 234–52, and reprinted in the third edition of *The Scouring of the White Horse* (London, 1889).

18. Donald O. Wagner, *The Church of England and Social Reform since 1854* (New York, 1930), p. 132.

19. J. Ewing Ritchie, *British Senators: Or, Political Sketches, Past and Present* (London: Tinsley, 1869), pp. 156, 151–52.

20. Introduction, *The Poetical Works of James Russell Lowell* (London, 1891), p. v.

21. For example, four of the chapter epigraphs in *Tom Brown's School Days* are from Lowell. But Hughes's citations from *The Biglow Papers* and other works by Lowell were not limited to his published writings. According to an early biographer of Lowell, Hughes "somewhat embarrassed the author of those poems by quoting from them on all occasions" (Horace E. Scudder, *James Russell Lowell* [Boston: Houghton Mifflin, 1901], 2:145).

22. See, e.g., *A Cycle of Adams Letters 1861–65*, ed. W. C. Ford (Boston: Houghton Mifflin, 1920), 1:45–46, 66; *Letters of Henry Adams (1858–1891)*, ed. W. C. Ford (Boston: Houghton Mifflin, 1930), pp. 95, 97; Moncure D. Conway, *Autobiography* (London: Cassell, 1904), 1:362; 2:1, 288.

23. Wendell Phillips Garrison and Francis Jackson Garrison, *William Lloyd Garrison 1805–1879* (New York: Century, 1889), 4:216.

24. The *Trent* was a British steamer that was stopped on the high seas by a Union vessel, the *San Jacinto*, in order to effect the forcible removal of two Confederate commissioners en route to England, James M. Mason and John Slidell.

25. This was also the name of the house Hughes bought for his mother in Rugby, Tennessee. She lived there from 1881 until her death in 1887. It still stands, under the care—like other structures on the colony site—of Historic Rugby, founded in 1966 as the Rugby Restoration Association.

26. *Spectator* 76 (March 28, 1896):435.

Chapter Two

1. *Tom Brown's School Days* (London: Macmillan, 1967), p. 56.

Subsequent references will be given parenthetically in the text. For convenience, because there are many editions in circulation, these will indicate the part (roman numeral) and chapter (arabic numeral), as well as the page(s) in this edition from Hughes's own publisher, Macmillan. This first quotation, e.g., would read: I, 3; 56.

2. Arthur's experience was apparently not uncommon. In a sermon on "Christian Responsibility" delivered in Rugby Chapel on April 11, 1841 (while Hughes was still a pupil), Arnold said, "It has been known ... that when young boys just come from home have knelt down at night to say their prayers, they have been interrupted, laughed at, annoyed for doing so" (*Christian Life* [London: Fellowes, 1849], p. 158).

3. *Edinburgh Review* 107 (January 1858):172.

4. Mack and Armytage, *Thomas Hughes*, pp. 90–91.

5. Sir Joshua Fitch, *Thomas and Matthew Arnold and Their Influence on English Education* (New York: Scribner, 1897), p. 105. In a letter to his mother Matthew Arnold said that his poem "Rugby Chapel" was inspired by Fitzjames Stephen's review of *Tom Brown's School Days* in the *Edinburgh Review*. The younger Arnold objected to Stephen's portrayal of his father as "a narrow bustling fanatic" and wished to correct it. See *The Letters of Matthew Arnold to Arthur Hugh Clough*, ed. Howard Foster Lowry (London: Oxford University Press, 1932), p. 164.

6. Newsome, *Godliness & Good Learning*, p. 37.

7. *Literary Gazette*, June 20, 1857, p. 587.

8. *Times* (London), October 9, 1857, p. 10. The term "muscular Christianity" first appeared in a review of Kingsley's *Two Years Ago* in the *Saturday Review* 4 (February 21, 1857):176.

9. See, e.g., Mack and Armytage, *Thomas Hughes*, p. 98.

10. Two of the antagonists mentioned here were in the news when the novel was published in 1857. The "Russians" had been in conflict with the English during the Crimean War (1854–56); and the "Border-ruffians," as we shall see in chapter 4, were proslavery guerrillas from Missouri who made bloody raids into Kansas until the end of the decade.

11. Introduction to *Tom Brown's School Days* (New York: Harper, 1911), p. x.

12. Ibid., p. xi.

13. *A Bibliographical Catalogue of Macmillan and Co.'s Publications from 1843 to 1889* (London: Macmillan, 1891), p. 60; Charles L. Graves, *Life and Letters of Alexander Macmillan* (London: Macmillan, 1910), pp. 120–21, 124.

14. *Saturday Review* 5 (December 11, 1858):589–90; and *Critic*, n. s. 17 (December 18, 1858):897–98.

15. Ian Yarrow, *Berkshire* (London: Hale, 1952), p. 105.

16. *The Scouring of the White Horse* (Cambridge, 1859 [1858]),

p. 19. Subsequent page references will be given parenthetically in the text.

17. For this view of Edmund as a hero Hughes probably drew on Carlyle's *Past and Present*; see especially II, 3, "Landlord Edmund."

18. For Macmillan's comment, see Graves, *Life and Letters*, p. 121. For Hughes on *Tom Brown's School Days* as "the first part of the present story," see the preface to *Tom Brown at Oxford* (London: Macmillan, 1883), p. vii. Subsequent page references will be given parenthetically in the text.

19. "School and College Life: Its Romance and Reality," *Blackwood's Edinburgh Magazine* 89 (February 1861):132, 143. For other early comments on the difference and decline in quality from *Tom Brown's School Days*, see *Examiner*, December 14, 1861, p. 792; *Saturday Review* 12 (December 14, 1861):611–13; and *Westminster Review*, n.s. 21 (January 1862):289–90.

20. *Critic*, n.s. 23 (November 23, 1861):517.

21. *Tom Brown's School Days* (London: Macmillan, 1880), p. xii.

22. In a whimsical essay the young P. G. Wodehouse professed to be so struck by the differences between Parts I and II of *Tom Brown's School Days* that he wondered if they could have been the work of two distinct authors. See "The Tom Brown Question," *Public School Magazine* 8 (December 1901):473–75. More seriously, Mack and Armytage suggest that while writing Part II Hughes was still saddened by the death of his eldest daughter (*Thomas Hughes*, p. 88).

Chapter Three

1. On mid-Victorian religious controversies, see Desmond Bowen, *The Idea of the Victorian Church* (Montreal: McGill University Press, 1968); Owen Chadwick, *The Victorian Church* (New York: Oxford University Press, 1966); A. O. J. Cockshut, *Anglican Attitudes* (London: Collins, 1959); Alec R. Vidler, *The Church in an Age of Revolution* (Grand Rapids: Eerdmans, 1962); Basil Willey, *Nineteenth Century Studies* (London: Chatto & Windus, 1949); and Basil Willey, *More Nineteenth Century Studies* (London: Chatto & Windus, 1956).

2. Willey, *More Nineteenth Century Studies*, p. 138.

3. *Edinburgh Review* 113 (April 1861):480.

4. Quoted in Mack and Armytage, *Thomas Hughes*, p. 120.

5. See, e.g., Maurice's letters to Stanley and Hughes in *The Life of Frederick Denison Maurice*, ed. Frederick Maurice (New York: Scribner, 1884), 2:382–83, 384–86.

6. The words are Ludlow's; *Life of Maurice*, 2:386–87.

7. *Religio Laici* (Cambridge, 1861), p. 9. Subsequent page references will be given parenthetically in the text.

8. The most famous use in English literature of the Latin version of this phrase, *religio laici*, was John Dryden's poem by that title (1682).

9. The Episcopal Church of Ireland was in fact disestablished in 1869, giving rise to the prospect that the Church of England would be next.

10. According to Chadwick, *Victorian Church*, "that amateur boxer and ex-socialist Tom Hughes" served for a time as one of the rector's bodyguards (p. 499).

11. *The Old Church; What Shall We Do With It?* (London, 1878), pp. 148–49. Subsequent page references will be given parenthetically in the text.

12. *The Manliness of Christ* (London, 1879), p. 93. Subsequent page references will be given parenthetically in the text.

13. Newsome, *Godliness*, argues that *The Manliness of Christ* shows how by the 1870s "Muscular Christianity was firmly establishing itself" in the place of "godliness and good learning" (p. 198). It is difficult to understand how a reading of the book could lead to this conclusion. Indeed, one early reviewer was relieved to discover that Christ's "'manliness' is *not* the old 'muscular Christianity,' only under a new name" (*Spectator* 53 [April 3, 1880]:438; emphasis added).

14. For a discussion of the place of the wreck of the *Birkenhead* in the Victorian imagination, see Mark Girouard, *The Return to Camelot* (New Haven, 1981), pp. 8, 13.

Chapter Four

1. "Opinion on American Affairs," *Macmillan's Magazine* 4 (September 1861):414. Subsequent page references will be given parenthetically in the text.

2. Donaldson Jordan and Edwin J. Pratt, *Europe and the American Civil War* (Boston: Houghton Mifflin, 1931), p. 13.

3. "The Struggle for Kansas," in J. M. Ludlow, *A Sketch of the History of the United States* (Cambridge, 1862), p. 321. Subsequent page references will be given parenthetically in the text.

4. "Latest Views of Mr. Biglow," 1. 45.

5. For reliable modern accounts, see chapter 5, "'Bleeding Kansas'—the Territorial Period," pp. 61–78, in Robert W. Richmond, *Kansas: A Land of Contrasts* (St. Charles, Mo.: Forum Press, 1974); and chapter 6, "Bleeding Kansas, 1854–1859," pp. 67–79, in William Frank Zornow, *Kansas: A History of the Jayhawk State* (Norman: University of Oklahoma Press, 1957).

6. Hughes is probably overstating his case here. As the *Encyclopedia of American History* (ed. Richard B. Morris [New York: Harper, 1961], p. 227) puts it, even if the two Democratic candidates, Stephen A. Doug-

las and John C. Breckenridge, and the Constitutional candidate, John Bell, had "combined on a fusion ticket," Lincoln would have lost only eleven electoral votes and been left with more than enough to win.

7. *Times* (London), January 19, 1863, p. 8.

8. *The Cause of Freedom* (London [1863]), p. 10. Subsequent page references will be given parenthetically in the text.

9. "Exeter Hall and Emancipation," *Saturday Review* 15 (January 31, 1863):141–42.

10. "'Peace on Earth,'" *Macmillan's Magazine* 13 (January 1866): 201. This article was published in the United States in pamphlet form by the Old South Work of Boston (Old South Leaflets, no. 181, n.d.).

11. Nelson F. Adkins, "Thomas Hughes and the American Civil War," *Journal of Negro History* 18 (July 1933):328, 329.

12. *Vacation Rambles* (London, 1895), p. 146.

13. Ibid., p. 169.

14. Ibid., p. 177. Cf. pp. 169–70, 178.

15. This speech was reprinted in *Macmillan's Magazine* 23 (December 1870):81–91; the following quotations are taken from that version.

16. Marguerite Bartlett Hamer, "Thomas Hughes and His American Rugby," *North Carolina Historical Review* 5 (October 1928):390–412; M. B. Hamer, "The Correspondence of Thomas Hughes Concerning His Tennessee Rugby," *North Carolina Historical Review* 21 (July 1944): 203–14; W. H. G. Armytage, "New Light on the English Background of Thomas Hughes' Rugby Colony in Tennessee," *East Tennessee Historical Society's Publications* 21 (1949):69–84; W. H. G. Armytage, "Public School Paradise," *Queen's Quarterly* 57 (Winter 1950–51):530–36; W. Hastings Hughes, *The True Story of Rugby*, ed. John R. DeBruyn (Jackson, Tenn.: n.p., n.d.); John R. DeBruyn, "Letters to Octavius Wilkinson: Tom Hughes' Lost Uncle," *Princeton University Library Chronicle* 34 (Autumn 1972):33–52; Brian L. Stagg, *The Distant Eden: Tennessee's Rugby Colony* (Rugby, Tenn.: Paylor Publications, 1973); W. H. G. Armytage, Introduction to Thomas Hughes, *Rugby, Tennessee* (London, 1881; repr. Philadelphia: Porcupine Press, 1975), 8 pp. unpaginated; and John R. DeBruyn, "Thomas Hughes on Eduard Bertz," *Notes and Queries*, n.s. 23 (September 1976):405–6.

17. Mack and Armytage, *Thomas Hughes*, p. 236.

18. "A Week in the West," *Macmillan's Magazine* 24 (August 1871):246.

19. *Rugby, Tennessee*, p. 117. Subsequent page references will be given parenthetically in the text.

20. Joseph Addison, *Spectator* No. 108, July 4, 1711.

21. Armytage, "New Light on the English Background," p. 76.

22. "Man the Reformer," *Essays and Poems of Emerson*, ed. Stuart P. Sherman (New York: Harcourt, Brace, 1921), p. 309.

23. Hamer, "Thomas Hughes and His American Rugby," p. 408.

Chapter Five

1. An English genealogist has traced Hughes's ancestry back through thirty-two generations to King Alfred. See Ivy M. Curzon, *Pedigree of Thomas Hughes, Q.C.* ([London: n.p., 1972]).

2. Graves, *Life and Letters*, p. 154.

3. *Vacation Rambles*, p. 145.

4. For an account of the "Sunday Library," see *Letters of Alexander Macmillan*, ed. George A. Macmillan ([Glasgow: printed for private circulation at the University Press, 1908]), pp. xxxvi–xxxvii. George Macmillan says that *Alfred the Great* was "still in regular demand" nearly forty years after its first publication.

5. At least one reviewer complained about Hughes's unsophisticated and inaccurate use of nineteenth-century scholarship; see *Saturday Review* 29 (April 30, 1870):582–84. For an overview of more recent scholarship concerning Alfred, see Eleanor Shipley Duckett, *Alfred the Great* (Chicago: University of Chicago Press, 1956), pp. 208–15.

6. *Alfred the Great* (London: Macmillan, 1898), p. 3. Subsequent page references will be given parenthetically in the text.

7. This is Lecture VI of Carlyle's *On Heroes, Hero-Worship and the Heroic in History* (1841).

8. The phrase appears in "The Present Time," the first of Carlyle's *Latter-Day Pamphlets* (1850). Hughes quotes a sentence from this, including a reference to "the God-made king," immediately after his opening quotation from *On Heroes*.

9. Hughes gives the date of Alfred's death as October 26, 901 (p. 301). Modern authorities, however, place it two years earlier; see, e.g., Duckett, *Alfred*, p. 197. Alfred was born in 849.

10. *Memoir of a Brother* (London, 1873), p. vii. Subsequent page references will be given parenthetically in the text.

11. In his *Marianne Thornton* (1956), E. M. Forster has shown how such documents can be skillfully worked into a biography of an obscure relative.

12. *Memoir of a Brother* did apparently enjoy considerable popular success when it appeared, going through seven printings in the first ten months after publication. Lowell wrote Hughes that he "read every word of it" the day he received it, staying up until 1:30 A.M. to do so; *Letters of James Russell Lowell*, ed. Charles Eliot Norton (New York: Harper, 1894), 2:92.

13. *Memoir of Daniel Macmillan* (London, 1883), p. ix. Subsequent page references will be given parenthetically in the text.

14. See *Letters of Alexander Macmillan*, pp. 319, 320, 321.

15. Charles Morgan in his centenary history of *The House of Macmillan* (New York: Macmillan, 1944) dismisses this reticence of Hughes's as "coyness" (p. 38), but Morgan's obvious contempt for Hughes does not prevent him from drawing heavily on the *Memoir of Daniel Macmillan* in writing his own book.

16. See Edward C. Mack, *Peter Cooper* (New York: Duell, Sloan and Pearce, 1949), pp. 385–86; and Allan Nevins, *Abram S. Hewitt* (New York: Harper, 1935), p. 452.

17. *Life and Times of Peter Cooper* (London, 1886), p. 8. Subsequent page references will be given parenthetically in the text. Nevins thought that Hughes mistakenly tried to give "the rugged industrial pioneer the flavor of a Dr. Arnold hero" (*Hewitt*, p. 452). What "a Dr. Arnold hero" might be is not immediately apparent, but it is clear that Hughes looked to Carlyle rather than to Arnold for his definition of a hero and that Carlyle recognized several different kinds, possibly including—if only they would follow his advice—modern industrialists. See his *Past and Present*, 4:4, "Captains of Industry."

18. Mack discusses these "Reminiscences" in his biography of Cooper, p. 386. A more succinct *Autobiography of Peter Cooper* was published posthumously by the Old South Work of Boston (Old South Leaflets, No. 147, n.d.). Hughes apparently did not see this in manuscript.

19. Letter from Hughes to Alexander Macmillan, February 27, 1886; quoted in Mack and Armytage, *Thomas Hughes*, p. 265.

20. *James Fraser* (London, 1887), p. 171. Subsequent page references will be given parenthetically in the text.

21. Livingstone was certainly aware of Hughes. On May 27, 1865, he wrote a friend: "I have been reading *Tom Brown's School Days*—a capital book" (William Garden Blaikie, *The Personal Life of David Livingstone* [London: John Murray, 1881], p. 355). William Cotton Oswell, an associate of Livingstone's in Africa whom the explorer greatly admired, had been one of Hughes's boyhood heroes at Rugby. See Hughes's "William Cotton Oswell," *Macmillan's Magazine* 70 (August 1894):307–12.

22. Richard D. Altick, *The English Common Reader* (Chicago: University of Chicago Press, 1957), p. 388.

23. Graves, *Life and Letters*, pp. 25–26, 355–56.

24. On two earlier occasions Hughes had written appreciative reviews for *Macmillan's Magazine* of books by another famous African explorer, Sir Samuel White Baker: *The Nile Tributaries of Abyssinia, and the Sword Hunters of the Hamran Arabs* (17 [December 1867]: 145–52); and *Ismailia: A Narrative of the Expedition to Central Africa*

for the Suppression of the Slave Trade (31 [December 1874]:99–107).
Both books were published by Macmillan.

25. That it is possible to both intelligible and perceptive in a brief
study of Livingstone has been demonstrated by Jack Simmons in his
Livingstone and Africa (London: English Universities Press, 1955). Like
Hughes's book, it appeared in a series of short volumes ("Teach Yourself
History") to which well-known authors contributed.

26. *David Livingstone* (London, 1889), p. 87. Subsequent page
references will be given parenthetically in the text.

27. Blaikie, *Personal Life*, p. 244.

28. Hughes quotes neither the entry for April 15 nor that for June
24 with complete accuracy, and both of them are considerably longer
than the excerpts that appear in Hughes's book. See *The Last Journals
of David Livingstone* (London: John Murray, 1874), pp. 177, 202–3.

29. Hughes calls Livingstone's surprise guest Henry Morland, rather
than Morton, Stanley (*David Livingstone*, p. 140); the error is not
entirely his, however, for in his source Livingstone gives Stanley's middle
name as Moreland (*Last Journals*, p. 156).

30. Blaikie, *Personal Life*, p. 417.

31. Livingstone, *Last Journals*, p. 287.

32. George Seaver (*David Livingstone* [London: Lutterworth Press,
1957]), while rejecting the "aura of hagiography" (p. 5) with which
many writers on Livingstone endow him, also expresses his gratitude that
Livingstone "escaped the brilliant but virulent pen of Lytton Strachey
whose caricatures of some Eminent Victorians set the vogue for future
less-gifted belittlers of human greatness" (p. 6). Seaver faces up to
Livingstone's defects, but he does not go nearly so far as, e.g., Oliver
Ransford, who gives the subtitle *The Dark Interior* to his *David Livingstone* (London: John Murray, 1978). This argues that Livingstone suffered from cyclothymia, a form of manic-depressive psychosis.

33. Lytton Strachey, *Eminent Victorians* (New York: Modern Library, n.d.), p. viii.

Chapter Six

1. "Arnold and His School," *North British Review* 28 (February
1858):139.

2. See, e.g., Richard Usborne, "A Re-reading of 'Tom Brown,'"
Spectator 197 (August 17, 1956):229; and Kenneth Allsop, "A Coupon
for Instant Tradition: On 'Tom Brown's Schooldays,'" *Encounter* 25 (November 1965):60–63.

3. There have been three film versions: in 1916, 1940, and 1951.
A five-part television series was shown on BBC-TV in 1971 and on the
American "Masterpiece Theatre" (PBS) in 1973.

Selected Bibliography

PRIMARY SOURCES

1. Novels

The Scouring of the White Horse. Cambridge: Macmillan, 1859 [1858].
Tom Brown at Oxford. Cambridge: Macmillan, 1861. Serialized in *Macmillan's Magazine,* November 1859–July 1861.
Tom Brown's School Days. Cambridge: Macmillan, 1857.

2. Biographies

Alfred the Great. London: Macmillan [1869].
David Livingstone. London: Macmillan, 1889.
James Fraser, Second Bishop of Manchester: A Memoir, 1818–1885. London: Macmillan, 1887.
Life and Times of Peter Cooper. London: Macmillan, 1886.
Memoir of a Brother. London: Macmillan, 1873.
Memoir of Daniel Macmillan. London: Macmillan, 1882.

3. Autobiographies

Early Memories for the Children. London: Thomas Burleigh, 1899. Also published as "Fragments of Autobiography," edited by Henry C. Shelley. *Cornhill Magazine,* n.s. 58 (March 1925):280–89; (April 1925):472–78; (May 1925):563–72.
"Thomas Hughes." In *True Manliness,* edited by E. E. Brown. Boston: D. Lothrop, 1880, pp. vi–xxii.
Vacation Rambles. London: Macmillan, 1895.

4. Other Nonfictional Works

Account of the Lock-Out of Engineers, &c. 1851–2. Cambridge: Macmillan, 1860.
Address [by His Honour Thos. Hughes, Q.C.,] on the Occasion of the Presentation of a Testimonial in Recognition of His Services to the Cause of Co-operation. Manchester: Co-Operative Printing Society, 1885.
The Cause of Freedom: Which Is Its Champion in America, The North or the South? London: Emancipation Society [1863].
Church Reform and Defence. London: Richard Clay [1886].

Co-Operative Faith and Practice (with E. Vansittart Neale). Manchester: Co-Operative Union [1890].

Co-Operative Production. Manchester: Central Co-Operative Board [1887].

Fifty Years Ago: A Layman's Address to Rugby School. London: Macmillan [1891].

History of the Working Tailors' Association. London: George Bell [1850].

King's College and Mr. Maurice. London: D. Nutt, 1854.

Lecture on the History & Objects of Co-operation. Manchester: Central Co-operative Board [1878].

A Lecture on the Slop-System, Especially As It Bears upon the Females Engaged in It. Exeter: Pollard, 1852.

The Manliness of Christ. London: Macmillan, 1879.

The Old Church; What Shall We Do With It? London: Macmillan, 1878.

Religio Laici. Cambridge: Macmillan, 1861. Reprinted as *A Layman's Faith.* London: Macmillan, 1868.

Rugby, Tennessee. London: Macmillan, 1881.

"The Struggle for Kansas." In J. M. Ludlow, *A Sketch of the History of the United States.* Cambridge: Macmillan, 1862, pp. 319–80.

5. Prefaces

G. T. T. Gone to Texas: Letters from Our Boys. Edited by Thomas Hughes. London: Macmillan, 1884, pp. v–xiii.

Kingsley, Charles. *Alton Locke.* London: Macmillan, 1876, pp. ix–lxi.

Lowell, James Russell. *The Biglow Papers.* Edited by Thomas Hughes. London: Trübner, 1859, pp. vii–xxxvi.

———. *The Poetical Works.* London: Macmillan, 1891, pp. v–xxxii.

A Manual for Co-operators. Edited by Thomas Hughes and E. Vansittart Neale. London: Macmillan, 1881, pp. iii–xvi.

Marriott, J. A. R. *Charles Kingsley, Novelist.* Oxford: Blackwell, 1892, pp. iii–v.

Maurice, Frederick Denison. *Christian Socialism.* Oxford: Christian Social Union [1898], p. 2.

———. *The Friendship of Books and Other Lectures.* London: Macmillan, 1880, pp. v–xxxiv.

Paris, Comte de. *The Trades' Unions of England.* Edited by Thomas Hughes. London: Smith, Elder, 1869, pp. vii–xiv.

Philpot, J. Harvey. *Guide Book to the Canadian Dominion.* London: Edward Stanford, 1871, pp. vii–xxxvi.

Whitmore, William. *Gilbert Marlowe, and Other Poems.* Cambridge: Macmillan, 1859, pp. iii–viii.

SECONDARY SOURCES

1. Books

Briggs, Asa. *Victorian People*. Chicago: University of Chicago Press, 1955. Chapter on Hughes's role, especially through *Tom Brown's School Days*, in molding national opinion about the public schools.

Girouard, Mark. *The Return to Camelot*. New Haven: Yale University Press, 1981. The contributions of Hughes, *Tom Brown's School Days*, and Christian Socialism to the revival of the chivalric ideal in Victorian England.

Haley, Bruce. *The Healthy Body and Victorian Culture*. Cambridge, Mass.: Harvard University Press, 1978. Chapter 7 contains an excellent analysis of *Tom Brown's School Days*.

Harrison, J. F. C. *A History of the Working Men's College 1854–1954*. London: Routledge & Kegan Paul, 1954. Includes an account of Hughes's contributions.

Mack, Edward C., and Armytage, W. H. G. *Thomas Hughes*. London: Ernest Benn, 1952. The only book-length biography, based on unpublished as well as published materials.

Masterman, N. C. *John Malcolm Ludlow*. Cambridge: Cambridge University Press, 1963. Much information about Hughes, including some from the Ludlow papers at Cambridge University.

Mayor, Stephen. *The Churches and the Labour Movement*. London: Independent Press, 1967. Hughes's exertions on behalf of social justice.

Newsome, David. *Godliness & Good Learning*. London: John Murray, 1961. Hughes's influence in propagating the cult of the body in late nineteenth-century England.

Parrish, Morris L., and Maun, Barbara Kelsey. *Charles Kingsley and Thomas Hughes*. London: Constable, 1936. First editions (and some later) of Thomas Hughes at Dormy House, Pine Valley, N.J. (now in the Princeton University Library).

Proctor, Mortimer. *The English University Novel*. Berkeley: University of California Press, 1957. *Tom Brown at Oxford* as an early example.

Reed, John R. *Old School Ties: The Public Schools in British Literature*. Syracuse: Syracuse University Press, 1964. The effect of *Tom Brown's School Days* in popularizing the English public schools.

Selfe, Sydney. *Notes on the Characters and Incidents Depicted by the Master Hand of Tom Hughes in "Tom Brown's Schooldays."* Rugby: A. J. Lawrence, 1909. Skeptical about claims that these "characters and incidents" had real-life originals. Expanded into *Chapters from the History of Rugby School. Together with Notes on the Characters and Incidents Depicted in Tom Brown's Schooldays*. Rugby: A. J. Lawrence, 1910.

Vidler, Alex R. *F. D. Maurice and Company*. London: SCM Press, 1966. Chapter on the background of *The Old Church*.

Wagner, Donald O. *The Church of England and Social Reform since 1854*. New York: Columbia University Press, 1930. An earlier study than Mayor's of Hughes's work as a social reformer in Parliament and outside.

2. Articles

Carter, J. "Some Letters of Thomas Hughes." *Economic Review* 24 (October 1914):381–88. Written in the 1890s, these show his interest in the new Christian Social Union and his fears for the future of the cooperative movement.

[Davies, J. Llewelyn.] "Hughes, Thomas." *Dictionary of National Biography. Supplement*. New York: Macmillan, 1901, 3:7–10. His life story as told succinctly by a personal friend and fellow–Christian Socialist.

Harrington, Henry R. "Childhood and the Victorian Ideal of Manliness in *Tom Brown's Schooldays*." *Victorian Newsletter*, no. 44 (Fall 1973):13–17. Hughes's version of manliness seen as "sexual energy" sublimated "into social, public commitment."

Harrison, Eric. "The Englishry of Tom Brown." *Queen's Quarterly* 50 (Spring 1943):37–52. The relevance of *Tom Brown's School Days* during World War II.

Hartley, A. J. "Christian Socialism and Victorian Morality: The Inner Meaning of *Tom Brown's School-days*." *Dalhousie Review* 49 (1969):216–23. The novel "as a social document depicting a polity in miniature as a model for national society."

Hibberd, Dominic. "Where There Are No Spectators: A Rereading of *Tom Brown's Schooldays*." *Children's Literature in Education* 21 (1976):64–73. The novel viewed by a modern Old Rugbeian not only as a piece of nostalgia but also as "a surprisingly tidy story."

Ludlow, J. M. "Thomas Hughes and Septimus Hansard. A Sequel." *Economic Review* 6 (July 1896):297–316. Account of Hughes by his closest friend among the Christian Socialists.

Maison, Margaret M. "Tom Brown and Company: Scholastic Novels of the 1850s." *English* 12 (Autumn 1958):100–103. The popularity of the schoolboy novel during the decade of *Tom Brown's School Days*.

Reed, John R. "The Public Schools in Victorian Literature." *Nineteenth-Century Fiction* 29 (June 1974):58–76. *Tom Brown's School Days* "entirely transformed public opinion about the schools."

Winn, William E. "*Tom Brown's Schooldays* and the Development of 'Muscular Christianity.'" *Church History* 29 (1960):64–73. Hughes as a "muscular Christian."

Index